Mediterranean Hot and Spicy

ALSO BY AGLAIA KREMEZI

The Foods of Greece

The Mediterranean Pantry

Mediterranean Hot

The Foods of the Greek Islands

Mediterranean Hot and Spicy

Healthy, Fast, and Zesty Recipes from
Southern Italy, Greece, Spain, the Middle East, and North Africa

Aglaia Kremezi

PHOTOGRAPHS BY ANASTASIOS MENTIS

BROADWAY BOOKS ✦ NEW YORK

PUBLISHED BY BROADWAY BOOKS

Published in the United States by Broadway Books,
an imprint of The Doubleday Publishing Group,
a division of Random House, Inc., New York.
www.broadwaybooks.com

Versions of some of the recipes were published previously in
The Mediterranean Pantry (Artisan, 1994) and *Mediterranean Hot* (Artisan 1996).

Book design by Elizabeth Rendfleisch
Photographs by Anastasios Mentis with the assistance of Aglaia Kremezi

Library of Congress Cataloging-in-Publication Data
Kremezi, Aglaia.
    Mediterranean hot and spicy : healthy, fast, and zesty recipes from Southern Italy,
Greece, Spain, the Middle East, and North Africa / Aglaia Kremezi ; photographs by
Anastasios Mentis.
        p. cm.
1. Cookery, 1822. 2. Cookery (Hot peppers) 3. Cookery (Spices) I. Title.
TX725.M35K735 2009
641.59182′2—dc22
2008029660

ISBN 978-0-7679-2745-1

PRINTED IN CHINA

10   9   8   7   6   5   4   3   2   1

First Edition

To Costas, my husband,

for his invaluable help and support.

His love of spicy food

has been an inspiration.

CONTENTS

PREFACE

This collection of recipes is the result of my love affair with hot and zesty Mediterranean food. These are the dishes I cook, the food I love to eat. They are inspired by age-old culinary traditions that evolved in home kitchens in southern Europe, North Africa, and the Middle East. Mediterranean women—not professional chefs—in their quest to find different ways to feed their families from garden crops conceived myriad flavorful and satisfying dishes with each season's produce. The traditional Mediterranean way of cooking is, first and foremost, true to the ingredients. It uses grains, legumes, vegetables, olive oil, fish, and a little meat and dairy to create food bursting with color, flavor, and aroma, spiked with the fragrant chiles of the area. Ingenious combinations of spices and herbs add an extra layer of flavor to even the simplest dishes. That this food has been proven to be healthful comes as a bonus. We knew it all along, but scientists have now confirmed that highly flavored and spicy hot dishes help us control the amount of food we consume. We eat less without feeling deprived. But that is hardly the reason I choose to cook with seasonal vegetables and spices. Flavor is, and always was, my main concern.

Spicy foods were part of my teenage rebellion. Strong *skordalia* (garlic sauce) was the most highly flavored food served in our house. My father considered spices unhealthy and "politically incorrect." I grew up at a time when urban Greeks were trying hard to be Westernized. The ubiquitous cumin and all other common spices were banished, regarded as unrefined and Eastern-influenced, associated with the years of Ottoman domination. According to my grandmother, only poor, ignorant peasants cooked the old traditional spicy dishes. She, like most city people—including chefs at fashionable Athenian restaurants of the time—tried to transform the old recipes in accordance with the rules of classic French cuisine, usually with disastrous results. Greece was not the only European-Mediterranean country with such a split personality in its use of spices. France and especially Italy shared similar views. Only in recent years have the "peasants" of the Italian South returned to celebrating their love of peperoncini, shedding the inferiority complex imposed on them by the "civilized" Italian North.

In my travels, I have found that parts of Italy, Spain, and Malta, as well as of Turkey, Tunisia, and Morocco, are culinary time capsules, where foods have been preserved exactly as described in ancient texts. Israel offered me an unexpected culinary experience. In restaurants, market food stands, and homes, I sampled much more than the rich Sephardic tradition; I found a splendid pan-Mediterranean cuisine. At the oriental meat restaurants (they offer mainly gyros or shawarma) and falafel stands I tasted fabulous hot sauces and condiments from all parts of the region. Thanks to the Jews who emigrated from Ethiopia and Yemen, the spicy cooking of those countries was also added to the Mediterranean palette. I was fascinated to see how the fiery *zhug*, for example, has already become a Mediterranean classic.

·   ·   ·

Choosing recipes is for me the most difficult part of creating a book, as it has been since I started writing my first, *The Foods of Greece,* in the early nineties. Developing recipes was the easiest thing, right from the start. My problem was deciding which of the numerous versions—which I could not stop inventing—to include. Today, after four books in English and six in Greek, the process is not getting much easier. But at least I have decided on a principle that helps: I focus on naturally grown seasonal ingredients and pick out dishes that showcase them in the simplest and purest way, leaving out unnecessary embellishments. I hope my recipes will inspire you to use the abundance of seasonal produce available in your area to prepare dishes with clear, vivid, and invigorating flavors.

ACKNOWLEDGMENTS

I can't thank Jennifer Josephy, my editor, enough for enthusiastically embracing my passion for spicy Mediterranean foods, for her encouragement, and for her patience with my far-from-perfect English. I am grateful to Chris Benton for her brilliant copyediting, to proofreader Maureen Clark, and to Stephanie Bowen and Anne Chagnot for being so accommodating and supportive. Many thanks to Elizabeth Rendfleisch, who designed the book and made it beautiful, and to Ada Yonenaka, Luisa Francavilla, Tammy Blake, Catherine Pollock, and the rest of the Broadway team.

My agent Sarah Jane Freymann, my best friend and intellectual coach, had the original idea for a small book about the spicy Mediterranean dishes I cook at home. Different versions of some of the recipes were published more than a dozen years ago. This collection has many new dishes from a region that still boasts a wealth of undiscovered culinary treasures. Having my own vegetable garden on the island of Kea has brought me even closer to age-old Mediterranean food traditions, and I would like to thank my neighbor Zinovia Stefa and my friend Stamatia Stylou for their advice and help.

I have been gathering recipes and ideas over many years—traveling, researching old and new books, and cooking with friends from neighboring countries. I would like to start by thanking my Turkish friends Ayfer Unsal and Filiz Hösukoglu from Gaziantep, and Zeki Yesilyurt, who has now opened his own restaurant in New York. Thanks to Anna Zammit from Malta, to Maria José Sevilla, and especially to José Andrés, the most talented chef I know, who gave me inside information about Spanish food. In North Africa I had the privilege to learn firsthand about Moroccan and Tunisian foods from my friend and mentor Paula Wolfert. She shared with me her deep knowledge and introduced me to many home cooks of the area. I can't thank Paula enough for her precious help and guidance. I am also grateful to Dunn Gifford and Sara Baer-Sinnot of Oldways Preservation and Exchange Trust for organizing memorable trips to North Africa and southern Europe.

I am most grateful to my soul mate Anissa Helou, the London-based Lebanese food writer and historian, who not only shared her recipes and deep knowledge of Arab and Middle Eastern cuisine and ingredients but also provided me with seeds for the fascinating herb zaatar, and deciphered the secrets of the wonderful spice blends of the region. Many Italian friends have helped me over the years with recipes and ideas: Princess Marina Colonna from Molise, Isabella Oztasciyan-Bernardini from Lecce, Rosella Speranza from Bari, and especially Mary Taylor Simeti, author and food historian, who knows Sicilian foods better than anyone. I am grateful to Salone del Gusto, the biennial Slow Food gastronomic exhibition in Turin. While sampling rare delicacies from all over the world, especially from all the regions of Italy, and meeting the people who made them I had the chance to encounter artisanal producers of various *salumi* and *salsiciotti* (small sausages) from

Calabria, who told me all I needed to know about the very flavorful fiery peperoncini.

My trip to Israel was an unforgettable experience, and I would like to express my deepest gratitude to fellow food writer Dalia Lamdani for taking me into homes and restaurants and to the most fascinating ethnic markets of Tel Aviv. Thanks also to Soshana Kabel and chefs Bino Gabso and Margaret Victor-Tayar for giving me recipes from their restaurants, and to my good friend Joan Nathan for introducing me to the new Israeli cuisine.

Last but not least, many thanks to Anastasios Mentis, the New York–based photographer who tirelessly worked sixteen-hour days here in Kea to photograph the dishes. His talent and determination to do the best, even under the most difficult conditions, were impressive. Both Anastasios and I would like to express our gratitude to Christina Morali and Vicki Snyder, the potters who gave us the exquisite plates featured in many pictures. Also, many thanks to friends and family who lent us their china and flatware, and to Peggy Sotirhos, who combed through flea markets and shops to find me the perfect rectangular plates.

INTRODUCTION

The Mediterranean, especially its eastern end, was home to the most ancient civilizations: Mesopotamians, Egyptians, Phoenicians, Jews, Greeks, Persians, Romans, and later Arabs and Ottomans inhabited those shores. Their culinary legacies remain apparent today, and in parts of North Africa and the Middle East the exact dishes described in ancient texts—foods that freely combine sweet and savory, fragrant and spicy flavors—can still be found.

Maybe that is, at least in part, because food was more than sustenance. According to ancient medicine, food was the major means of preserving health in those who were well and restoring strength in those who were not. This was a theory that prevailed in medicine, both folk and formal, from the time of Hippocrates until the seventeenth century. In those days, in fact, most Greek, Latin, and Arab manuscripts and books about food also included medical recommendations—some completely strange and others interesting and sensible.

It was certainly sensible to add a multitude of herbs and spices to the gruels, soups, and hard, heavy flat breads people lived on. Domestic herbs and imported spices not only improved flavor but supposedly also provided the body with therapeutic and prophylactic substances. Spices and herbs were also believed to be aphrodisiacs, enhancing sexual potency. Many of the classic spice mixtures of the East contain ingredients that add no significant flavor or aroma but do contribute to "Adam's health," as an Ethiopian spice merchant told me in describing a mysterious grain that he insisted was part of the classic

Berber mixture ras el hanout. In its old form, the magical and aromatic Moroccan spice mixture (see page 13) contained *cantharides* (Spanish fly), the bright green little bugs that we now know are hazardous to health. In the old days, the often severe bladder irritation they caused was mistaken for sexual arousal.

Because they produce a burning sensation, spices like pepper, ginger, and chiles were associated with love and passion all over the Mediterranean and beyond. All hot spices were considered aphrodisiacs by the Romans (and also the Aztecs). Some medieval monasteries banned hot spices from the diets of chaste religious men. *Pili-pili* is the word for chile in Swahili and is also slang for the male sex organ, writes Amal Naj in his book *Peppers: A Story of Hot Pursuits.* There very well may be something to the association of hot spices with sex. Science has proven that the burning, almost painful sensation inflicted by pepper and chiles stimulates the brain to produce endorphins. These natural pain-killers create a euphoric feeling, a kind of high, which probably enhances sexual performance.

In view of these flavor-, health-, and passion-enhancing properties, it is not hard to understand why wars were waged, expensive and dangerous expeditions launched, lives lost, citizens enslaved, the landscape of faraway countries altered, and the map of the world changed, all in the name of keeping Europe supplied with spices. Exotic flavorings and aromatics became much more than condiments. European aristocrats and all others who could afford to do so paid fortunes to acquire these status symbols, the new hot currency replacing gold or silver and exchanged for other goods, even given as ransom.

For centuries Arabs were the only merchants who knew where pepper and the other precious aromatics came from. Spreading frightening tales about the strange creatures that guarded the spice trees in the countries beyond the Arab peninsula, they managed to keep their sources secret. Eventually, however, the Portuguese and Spaniards defeated the Arabs and took over the lucrative trade, discovering the New World in their quest for easier routes to the far-off lands of spice.

Ironically, the chile, one of the many plants brought from the New World, made the spicy taste accessible to the masses, putting an end to the spice craze of the European gentry. As anthropologist Sophie Coe, in her marvelous book *America's First Cuisines,* wrote, "The chili plant may have contributed to the disappearance of the powerfully spiced status dishes of the Renaissance and Baroque. The chili was cheap and easy to grow. It did not have to be imported from across the seas, passing from rapacious middleman to rapacious middleman and increasing in price every time it changed hands. Not being expensive, it could not be a status symbol. Peasants in a decent Mediterranean climate could grow it and feast on flavors their ancestors could not have afforded to dream of." At the beginning of the seventeenth century, the role played by spices, as luxury foods and status symbols, was taken

over by coffee, tea, chocolate, and sugar. At that time, the French developed a cuisine based on elaborate but very moderately spiced dishes, and the rest of Europe followed, transforming the flavor of Western cuisine and making it largely what it is today.

In North Africa and the Middle East, spices never went out of fashion, but feelings about spicy dishes in the European part of the Mediterranean are strong and contradictory. Italians of the North rarely hide their contempt for the hot foods of Calabria and other parts of the Italian South, considering them peasant and unrefined, as I mentioned before. Similarly, the Greek middle and upper classes have deliberately stripped the traditional cuisine of all spices. My father wasn't the only one who looked upon cumin and other "oriental flavorings" as hateful remnants of Greece's four-hundred-year Ottoman domination.

But things are changing. In recent years many Europeans, well-known and established French chefs among them, have been enthusiastically embracing the exhilarating aromas and flavors of the East. In other words, they are rediscovering the ingredients, tastes, and foods their ancestors were so eager to banish. Fortunately, parts of the Mediterranean kept the culinary traditions. Women who learned to cook from their mothers and grandmothers never stopped cooking the fragrant and zesty age-old foods. The recipes I collected in this book are based on these traditional spicy recipes.

THE ELEMENTS of MEDITERRANEAN CUISINE

Unlike classic French cuisine, the traditional cooking of the Mediterranean has no use for carefully prepared reductions, elaborate sauces, and sophisticated techniques. The plants and trees of the region, the domesticated animals, and the riches of the sea provide the elements essential to creating flavorful dishes. Home cooks inventively treat with respect even the most humble garden crop, creating simple, unembellished dishes that are delicious and healthy. Although there are differences among the various ethnic cuisines—between the Middle East and Spain, for example, or the Italian South and the North of Africa—there are also important common threads that link the foods of the region.

The Mediterranean regional cuisines are ingredient based, making the best of the produce of each season, creatively combining and complementing them to produce many different dishes. Most of the vegetables we consume today are native to the Mediterranean region and were first cultivated here: asparagus (the word is actually prehistoric), mushroom, beet (red and white), radish, turnip, carrot, parsnip, leek, cabbage, lettuce, artichoke, cucumber, fava bean, pea, onion, and garlic. Apart from cultivated vegetables, the wild leafy greens gathered from the hills or the mountains and the comestible weeds gleaned from the fields have filled an important role in the everyday diet since antiquity. On the other hand, tomatoes—considered an essential Mediterranean ingredient today—were imported from the New World by Columbus and only in the

mid-eighteenth century started to be cultivated extensively as food in Italy and later in other European countries. As far as we know, a recipe for pasta with tomato sauce first appeared in 1839.

Olive oil was and still is the main fat used by the inhabitants of the Mediterranean. While cheeses have been produced since antiquity, only when the Arabs conquered vast parts of the area—in the seventh and eighth centuries—did the use of dairy fats spread. Bernard Lewis, in his brilliant essay about the history of Middle Eastern food, entitled "The Finger Zone" (*New York Review of Books,* May 23, 2002), points out that in the old texts "etymology can be either misleading or instructive. In Hebrew *lehem* means bread, whereas the Arabic *lahm* means meat. Both obviously derive from the same word, and designate a major foodstuff, but not the same foodstuff. Similarly, *samn* in Arabic means clarified butter; the cognate Hebrew word *shemen* means oil. A moment's thought is enough to explain the difference. For the pastoral Arabs, these basic words designated meat and butter; for the agricultural Hebrews, bread and oil."

Grains were and still are the staple food all over the region. Breads and pitas of various forms, bulgur and polenta, pasta and couscous play a key role at the daily table. Complemented with seasonal vegetables and small amounts of fresh or cured meat or fish, the various breads or pastas provide nourishment and satisfy, as they become the canvas on which the incredible creativity of the Mediterranean home cooks is expressed.

Abundant homegrown or imported herbs, flavorings, and spices, wisely chosen and expertly combined, are the decisive brush-strokes that turn the simply prepared foods into memorable dishes that burst with flavor as they celebrate the season's best produce.

Unlike the tailor-made diets that come and go—the low-carb is only the latest of those fads—the Mediterranean way of eating is a traditional age-old regimen by which many generations have lived and prospered. Now that everybody in the United States can get flavorful naturally grown seasonal pro-duce, you don't need to go to southern Italy or Morocco to feast on incredibly tasty foods that are also healthy.

A Well-Stocked Mediterranean Pantry

HERBS, FLAVORINGS, AND SPICES

Spices are central to the *souks,* the picturesque markets of North Africa and the Middle East. Sacks full of dark red or brick-colored sweet and hot paprika, bright yellow turmeric pow-der, fragrant cinnamon, cardamom, cumin, and cloves, saffron threads or mari-gold leaves—its cheaper substitute—dried roots, and other aromatics are displayed in fascinat-ing abundance. The quantities startle unsus-pecting Westerners used to purchasing spices in tiny boxes and jars from the supermarket.

In fact, picking spices from the super-market shelves, although convenient, is not the best way to obtain the finest products. In many North American cities Middle Eastern and Asian markets sell a variety of spices. Those are the best places to look for fresher and fragrant products. There are also lots of Web sites where you can order even the most esoteric flavorings and spices (see Sources).

When buying spices, don't rely on appearance; looks can often be deceiving. Trust your sense of smell and taste. Buy whole spices and grind small quantities in a spice grinder, in a mortar, or in a clean coffee grinder. If you happen to find exceptionally good spices, buy larger quantities and freeze them in airtight containers. Cooking with spices requires practice, imagination, and a well-stocked spice shelf. The amounts suggested in the recipes are just starting points for your own experimentation. The taste, pungency, and aroma of each spice, or spice mixture, vary according to the country of origin, the freshness, the method of drying, and so forth.

Here are (in alphabetical order) some of the herbs, flavorings, and spices called for in the recipes. I start with the chiles and peppers, and their fascinating journey around the globe before they became such an important Mediterranean ingredient. I also include black pepper and its various forms and garlic, because I want to stress the seasonal characteristics of this ubiquitous Mediterranean ingredient.

Chiles and Peppers of the Mediterranean: As was the case with tomatoes and other plants imported to the Old Country from the New World, chiles were at first cultivated as ornamental plants. People admired the vividly colored fruits, the small chiles, but considered them poisonous. The eighteenth-century French philosopher Denis Diderot and General Lafayette of the American Revolution were both very suspicious of the hot fruits of the capsicum, stating that although the Indians of the New World ate them, no European could ever get used to their fiery taste.

The chiles of the Americas were first cultivated as condiments outside their place of origin on the western coast of Africa, not in Spain or Portugal. From West Africa—a stopover of the Portuguese ships returning from the New World—the chiles spread to the western coast of India, then to Macao in China, and from there to the Philippines, Japan, and the Spice Islands. In all those places the native populations found in chile the ideal cheap condiment for their foods. Traveling full circle, the chiles came back to America with the slaves from Africa, on board English and Dutch ships.

When finally the chile began to be considered a condiment in Europe—about fifty years from the time it was first brought from the New World—it was associated with India, where most of the spices came from. The German professor of medicine Leonard Fuchs, who was one of the first to draw botanical illustrations of the chile plant, named it "Calicut pepper," from the Indian city we call Calcutta today. In the fifteenth century, when the Ottomans invaded India, they brought the chiles back to Europe, distributing them throughout their vast empire, which included North Africa, the Middle East, and the Balkans. Turks liked

chile and introduced its cultivation to Bulgaria and Serbia, to northern Greece, and later to Hungary. The "Turkish pepper," as it was then called, led to the creation of paprika, the most important product of Hungary to this day. Through careful selection the seeds of the less hot peppers were collected and planted, gradually creating peppers that were not at all hot or just mildly hot, but very flavorful, which are used for the production of Hungarian paprika. Another sweet variety makes the delicious Spanish sweet and smoky *pimentón,* while the ñora peppers that are sold dry add deep flavor to romesco sauce (page 16) and lots of other Spanish dishes. According to an old Spanish belief, God created the sweet peppers, and the devil twisted them and made the fiery hot ones; in fact exactly the opposite happened.

In America, there is a clear distinction among the different kinds of chiles and their particular flavors, but around the Mediterranean—and throughout Europe—chiles are distinguished only by their heat level. The sunny and mostly dry climate of the Mediterranean makes very tasty hot and sweet peppers. What Italians call *peperoncini* (small peppers) are the hot chiles used most in the cooking of Sicily and Calabria. Peperoncini are closely related to the cayenne, but they are not tongue burning, and besides heat they have a deep fruity flavor and aroma. Pickled peperoncini, not the dry ones, are commonly available in the United States. Chile de árbol is a good substitute for the dry peperoncini in most recipes.

Piment d'Espelette is the ground sun-dried

chile grown in particular regions of the French Basque country. These are probably the most expensive European hot peppers, with DOC status. In most parts of Spain sweet or mildly hot peppers are ubiquitous, but in the Canary Islands, and occasionally in Estremadura and Galicia, the fiery small *guindillas* spike up various dishes.

Aleppo pepper, crushed dried Middle Eastern red peppers from the eponymous Syrian city, is less hot than Mexican chiles and more flavorful and fruity. Turkish Maraş peppers are similar to Aleppo but hotter, while Urfa peppers, from the eponymous region of southern Turkey, are usually moderately hot, with an exceptionally deep flavor. Bear in mind that the flavor and heat of Middle Eastern peppers vary from one year to the next. Their production is artisanal and, according to my Turkish friends, depends on the weather conditions—the amount of sun, rain, and other elements. Aleppo and the Turkish pepper can be bought at Middle Eastern shops (see Sources). If you buy a large quantity, store it in a sealed jar in the refrigerator. You can substitute about half the amount of ordinary hot red pepper flakes for Aleppo pepper or, better, a combination of hot red pepper flakes and some good flavorful Hungarian paprika.

Cilantro (fresh coriander): Also known as "Chinese parsley," this is an essential Asian herb, ubiquitous in Indian, Southeast Asian, and South American dishes. Cilantro is native to the Mediterranean and was probably introduced to India by Alexander the Great.

Both seeds and leaves were added to foods by ancient Greeks and Romans, and as today, people either loved it or hated it.

Garlic: The Mediterranean is definitely a garlic zone. Together with onions, fresh or sautéed garlic is the basis of most dishes. Today we take garlic for granted, but not so long ago the civilized northern Europeans and Americans looked upon Italian, Spanish, or Greek garlic eaters as unrefined peasants and second-class citizens. Ancient Greeks considered garlic an indispensable condiment with important therapeutic powers, something modern scientists have found to be true. All garlic is not created equal, and there is good reason why some heads are more sought after and pricier than others. In general, Italian and southern European garlic has smaller cloves and stronger flavor than Asian or American garlic. The mild green fresh garlic of the spring—available at many farmers' markets and specialized stores—is wonderful eaten raw in salads and spreads. In early summer, the plump, almost translucent, crunchy cloves of the newly formed young garlic heads are sweet and fragrant, while later, as summer progresses and the heads begin to dry, the flavor of the cloves concentrates and intensifies. Depending on the kind of garlic you have at hand, use more or fewer cloves for the recipes.

Herbs—Fresh Versus Dried: There is a big difference in flavor and aroma between fresh and dried oregano, cilantro (the leaves of fresh coriander) and coriander seeds, and fresh and dried mint. In Mediterranean cooking, dried herbs are usually used in stews and all kinds of cooked or baked dishes, while fresh herbs are added to salads, spreads, and occasionally marinades. There are many exceptions to that rule, of course. A small pinch of the dried wild Greek oregano—now imported to the United States—goes a long way; its potent aroma permeates meat and vegetable dishes, but it particularly shines sprinkled over feta cheese, and it miraculously transforms a simple olive oil and lemon dressing into the perfect sauce for grilled fish and seafood. Dried mint is a Middle Eastern essential, added to meatballs, to many spice blends, and to vegetable and yogurt spreads. It is steeped in boiling water to make the favorite tea of North Africa. Fresh mint is added to salads and stuffings, as well as to some sauces and dressings. Dried mint is not always readily available, but you can easily dry a bunch of fresh mint sprigs, hanging them upside down in a dry place. When completely dry, crumble the leaves and keep in an airtight jar in a cabinet away from heat.

Mahlep: The small seeds of a wild cherry, the size of apple seeds, mahlep gives a sweet and smoky aroma to breads and other baked goods. The grains should be the color of café au lait; dark brown grains indicate that the spice is old and probably stale. Mahlep is sold in Middle Eastern stores (see Sources). Buy it whole, not ground. Keep it in sealed jars in the freezer and grind small quantities as needed.

Mastic: This is the crystallized sap of the mastic shrub (*Pistacia lentiscus*), a kind of wild pistachio that grows only on southern Chios Island. Sweet with somewhat bitter undertones, it has an elusive, slightly turpentine aroma that cleanses the mouth. Very popular in the Arab countries and the Middle East, mastic is used as a flavoring, mainly in sweets, ice cream, breads, and drinks. Mastic was the chewing gum of ancient people, hence our word *masticate*. Mastic is sold in Middle Eastern and ethnic grocery stores (see Sources); store it in the freezer. When grinding it in a spice grinder, always mix the crystals with the sugar and the other spices used in the recipe to prevent the heat of the motor from melting the mastic, which could stick to the blades of the grinder.

Nigella: These tiny black seeds have a licorice-like flavor and aroma, similar to aniseeds. They are used as a topping or mixed into dough for breads and crunchy savory biscuits. Although they are sometimes called "black cumin" or "black sesame seeds," nigella seeds come from *Nigella sativa,* a plant not related to either of the two. They are sold at Middle Eastern and Indian grocery and spice shops (see Sources). Aniseeds or caraway seeds, or a combination, can be substituted.

Olive Oil: Greece is the country that uses more olive oil per capita than any other in the world—about $5^1/2$ gallons per person each year. The basic fat called for throughout this book is olive oil, and I always use Greek, which can often be found at a reasonable price in the United States. I do not specify extra virgin in all the recipes. I believe it is a waste to pay a lot of money for a fruity olive oil that will lose its distinctive taste when cooked. Extra virgin olive oil is essential only when it is used unheated, as in dressings and spreads.

Parsley and Celery: Flat-leaf parsley is used all over the Mediterranean. Its flavor is more prominent and aromatic than that of the curly parsley, which is rare in this part of the world. Mediterranean or French celery is the thin-stalked, dark green leafy plant that Americans call "wild celery." Although it does grow wild, most of it is cultivated. This fragrant celery has a strong taste, with a slight bitter undertone, so use it sparingly. It can be found in Asian markets under the name *kun choi* or *kin tsai*. You can also grow your own in the garden or in pots (for seeds, see Sources). If you come across it at a farmers' market, buy a lot, wash it well, coarsely chop it, and store in resealable plastic bags in the freezer, where it will keep for about six months. Thick-stalked American celery can be substituted, but its taste is much milder.

Peppercorns: Always buy whole peppercorns. Black peppercorns are dried unripe green berries that have fermented for a few days. Black pepper is fragrant and hot and should be ground at the last minute, just before use. Several varieties—such as the strong and pungent Tellicherry and the more subtle Malabar—are available at good spice shops. As a general rule get the best quality—uniform hard peppercorns without twigs. Whole peppercorns will keep for years, so it is worth buying in quantity. White peppercorns are skinned dried ripe peppercorns. White pepper is more pungent, less fragrant, and more expensive. I use it only to flavor white sauces, soups, and sometimes sweets. I much prefer the more complex taste of black pepper for most dishes. Green peppercorns, which are milder, are unripe corns preserved in brine or freeze-dried. Pink peppercorns (*Schinus molle*) are not related to pepper at all. They belong to a completely different species—distantly related to sumac. Pink peppercorns are very fragrant with a sour aftertaste, not pungent or hot. They can be crushed easily and are used for their aroma, mainly in dressings and sauces.

Pomegranate Molasses: Made from a special kind of sour pomegranates, this thick amber-colored syrup has a unique sour-sweet flavor. It is used in salad dressings and in meat and fish sauces throughout the Middle East and in Iran.

Rosebuds: Small, dried, fragrant rosebuds, as well as rose water, are popular flavorings, and not just for sweets. They are added to spice mixtures that flavor meat stews in some Mediterranean countries—especially in the Maghreb (Arab North Africa). Olive oil scented with roses was listed on clay tablets dating from about the thirteenth century B.C., found in the palaces of Knossos, Crete. Although it is not clear whether the ancient Greeks used that oil in foods or as a cosmetic, we do know that the Byzantines liked to add rose water along with *garum,* a fermented fish sauce, to their meat and game dishes.

Sumac: The ground tangy deep red fruits of the sumac bush (*Rhus coriaria*) are sprinkled over yogurt sauces, on spreads, as well as on onion and other salads. In the old days cooks used to steep whole dried sumac fruits in water and use the liquid as flavoring. Sumac is part of the large wild pistachio family. One very close relation is the Italian *lentiscus (skinos* in Greek), a shrub with small, hard, and very fragrant leaves that grows in clusters on the most dry and rocky Mediterranean shores.

Thyme (the herb za'atar): The subject of the various za'atar spice blends (see page 14) and the confusion about the exact type of thyme used in them get more knotty with the addition of yet another kind of fresh thyme, also called *za'atar* in Arabic. It is not a perennial and was probably gathered wild in the old days, together with other aromatic herbs. Now Middle Easterners plant it every year in their gardens. Its vivid green pointy leaves, larger than the leaves of common thyme, are eaten fresh all over the Arab countries. The fragrant sprigs are added to salads and occasionally flavor summer stews and marinades for grilled meat, fish, and vegetables. My friend the food writer Anissa Helou brought me seeds from Lebanon, and I planted them in my garden. The fresh za'atar-thyme that sprouted in late April grew into a very attractive shrub. The leaves have an addictive lemony, aromatic, and slightly spicy

taste. It was a revelation for me, and I wonder why it is not more widely known and used.

Turmeric: The deep yellow powder has a musky and earthy aroma when freshly ground but must be used sparingly because of its bitter undertones. Often called "Indian saffron" because it is used as a cheap saffron substitute, although the only common characteristic it shares with the precious stigmas of saffron is the yellow color. Turmeric is a rhizome related to and looking very much like ginger, but it has bright orange flesh. It is a native of Southeast Asia, and although recently it has occasionally been available fresh at some specialty markets, it is commonly used dried and powdered in North Africa and the Middle East. Scientists have recently found that it has antioxidant and some antimicrobial properties, probably preventing salmonella food poisoning.

Wild Fennel (*Finocchio selvatico*): The intensely aromatic wild fennel grows all over the Italian South and, fortunately, all over Greece. Its thick fronds add sweetness and aroma to Pasta con le Sarde (page 166), the great pasta dish of Sicily. In mainland Greece and in the islands wild fennel is added to pies made with spinach or other greens, to stuffings for summer vegetables and grape leaves, and to the marinade for raw sardines and anchovies (a kind of Mediterranean ceviche). You can only occasionally find wild fennel in the United States. A combination of fennel bulb, fronds, and freshly crushed fennel seeds is a good substitute.

DO-AHEAD
SPICE BLENDS,
SAUCES,
and
CONDIMENTS

During the late summer weekends,
when local tomatoes are at their best,
or in the spring and early summer,
when you find wonderful organic
lemons, very fragrant herbs, or
flavorful peppers and chiles, use them
to prepare sauces, jellies, pastes, and
rubs. Along with the recipes in this
chapter, do-ahead pantry items
include the crunchy savory and sweet
biscotti in the Breads and Desserts
chapter.

   During busy weeknights, the sauces
and condiments, spice and nut
blends, and spreads and flavorings
made with the best produce of each
season will help you whip up unusual
and original appetizers or an
authentic Mediterranean dinner in
twenty minutes.

✦ Bread Spice Mixture ✦

This is the mixture of spices I keep in a jar in the freezer to add extra flavor to any kind of bread—white, whole wheat, multigrain, as well as the breads I make with mashed pumpkin or greens. People love the aroma these spices give my loaves and flat breads. I also bake breads topped with olives, cheese, or just olive oil, garlic, and unprocessed salt crystals that we collect from the rocks. Makes about 1 cup

Uses: Add 2 to 3 teaspoons for each 4 cups flour you use in the bread recipe.

2/3 cup coriander seeds

4 teaspoons mahlep

1 teaspoon mastic crystals

2 tablespoons cumin seeds

Grind all the spices in a mortar, spice grinder, or clean coffee grinder to a powder. Transfer to an airtight container and keep in the freezer for up to 6 months.

✦ Baharat ✦

There are as many variations of this all-purpose spice blend—the word *baharat* means simply "spice" in Arabic—as there are cooks in the Arab countries. The ingredients, as well as the proportions, vary greatly from Lebanon to Turkey and from Tunisia to Syria. Use the optional ingredients or not, add or subtract elements, increase or decrease amounts of the spices—all to your taste. Makes about $^1/2$ cup

Uses: A few tablespoons of powdered baharat give depth of flavor to meat stews and stuffings. Rub pork, lamb, or any meat or poultry with the blend before grilling. Sprinkle on sparingly at the end of cooking to add an extra dimension and aroma to finished dishes.

3 or 4 dried edible rosebuds, stems discarded

2 tablespoons black peppercorns

Two 1-inch cinnamon sticks

2 tablespoons cumin seeds

2 tablespoons coriander seeds

5 or 6 cloves

1 teaspoon freshly grated nutmeg

2 or 3 cardamom pods (optional)

1 tablespoon dried mint (optional)

Good pinch of saffron threads (optional)

1 teaspoon grated lemon zest (optional)

Grind all the ingredients in a spice grinder or clean coffee grinder to a powder. Transfer to an airtight container and store for up to 1 month.

✦ Ras el Hanout ✦

Its name means "top of the shop," and it is the most enchanting of all Arab spice mixtures. The original old Moroccan blend contained no fewer than twenty-three different spices, aromatics, and aphrodisiacs, including the banned Spanish fly. Although you will find ground ras el hanout in specialty stores, I suggest you grind your own to make sure that your blend has the right heat and aroma.

Makes about 2 1/2 tablespoons

Uses: Flavor meat stews and stuffings or add a few tablespoons to olive oil to make a rub for grilled meat and poultry.

1 teaspoon cumin seeds

1 thumbnail-sized piece dried ginger, or 1 teaspoon ground

2 teaspoons coriander seeds

1 1/2 teaspoons black peppercorns

1/4 teaspoon cayenne

2 cloves

6 allspice berries

1 1/2 teaspoons ground cinnamon

Grind all the spices in a spice grinder or clean coffee grinder to a powder. Transfer to a small airtight container and store for up to 3 days.

✦ Za'atar ✦

The sweet flavor of toasted sesame seeds is wonderfully complemented by the red sour-tart ground fruits of sumac in this classic Arab spice mixture. There are many versions of the blend throughout the Middle East: The green Lebanese za'atar consists of toasted sesame seeds mixed with just thyme—dried before it blooms—and sumac. In Syria the gold-colored blend may have more spices—cumin, paprika, caraway, among others. The particular kind of Lebanese thyme—*za'atar* in Arabic—is an herb different from the Greek or the European common thyme or the hyssop that you will see listed in some recipes for the spice mixture. In fact, it is closer in shape and aroma to a thick-leaf oregano that grows in the Greek islands. As this kind of thyme is not available in the United States, I prefer to use a combination of dried thyme and savory. But as with all spice mixtures, the ingredients and proportions are a matter of taste, so feel free to experiment with the variations, additions, and substitutions you prefer.

Makes about 1 cup

Uses: Mix 1 to 2 tablespoons with 2 to 3 tablespoons extra virgin olive oil and spread on warm toasted bread or pita. Top with Maraş or Aleppo pepper or freshly ground black pepper to taste. I particularly like to top homemade flat bread or frozen pizza dough with the za'atar paste just before baking the thin breads in a very hot oven, on the barbecue, or on a griddle.

$^1/_2$ cup dried Mediterranean thyme, or
  $^1/_4$ cup dried Mediterranean savory and
  $^1/_4$ cup dried Mediterranean thyme

$^1/_4$ cup sumac

$^1/_2$ teaspoon coarse sea salt

1 teaspoon cumin seeds (optional)

$^1/_4$ cup plus 1 tablespoon sesame seeds, toasted (see page 213)

Grind the thyme or thyme and savory, sumac, salt, cumin if you're using it, and toasted sesame seeds in a spice grinder or clean coffee grinder almost to a fine powder. Or grind the spices and add the toasted sesame seeds. Store in a sealed jar in a cool, dark, dry place for up to 2 months.

✦ Dukkah ✦

There are countless versions of this hearty, aromatic Egyptian nut and spice blend, which is very easy to make. Besides sesame seeds, some blends include almonds, pistachios, or hazelnuts, while some of the oldest versions used ground roasted chickpeas, like the ones you will find in Greek and Turkish or Indian markets. The proportion of coriander and cumin seeds can also vary greatly—from 2 to 3 tablespoons to $1/2$ cup for each cup of nuts. Makes about $3^1/2$ cups

Uses: Mix 1 to 2 tablespoons with 2 to 3 tablespoons extra virgin olive oil and spread on warm toasted bread or pita. If you like, sprinkle with Maraş or Aleppo pepper. You can also top frozen or homemade pizza dough with dukkah and olive oil before baking in the oven or on a griddle.

Sprinkle dukkah over green salads (lettuce or mesclun) or over steamed cabbage, cauliflower, and broccoli.

Mix dukkah with bulgur to make Spicy Bulgur Salad with Nuts and Tomato Paste Dressing (page 78), a salad/main course ideal for picnics or buffet dinners.

Sprinkle *dukkah* over creamy yogurt or on cooked spaghetti tossed with garlicky oil and peperoncini to make an irresistible fast meal.

$2/3$ cup sesame seeds, toasted (see page 213)

1 cup coriander seeds, toasted (see page 213)

$1/2$ cup cumin seeds, toasted (see page 213)

1 teaspoon salt, preferably unprocessed rock salt (see Sources) or fleur de sel, or less to taste

$1^1/4$ cups hazelnuts, almonds, or a combination, toasted (see page 213)

$1/2$ to $1^1/2$ teaspoons freshly ground black pepper, to taste

Briefly grind the sesame, coriander, and cumin seeds with the rock salt if you're using it in a spice grinder or clean coffee grinder until coarsely ground. You don't want to make a paste.

In a blender or food processor, grind the nuts, turning the motor on and off, to get a somewhat fine consistency. Add the ground spices and pepper to taste, along with the finer salt if you're using it, and turn the motor on again for just 1 second. You want to make a dry, mealy dukkah, not an oily paste. Store in a sealed jar in a cool, dark, dry place for up to 3 months.

Catalan Roasted Tomato Sauce with Peppers and Nuts

I have no doubt that this sauce will one day be found in every supermarket in America," writes renowned chef José Andrés in his wonderful book *Tapas* . I am sure that when you taste romesco, you will agree with José. The fundamental difference between romesco and the more common tomato sauces is that in the Catalan sauce all the vegetables are baked in the oven, acquiring a sweeter caramelized flavor that is balanced with good sherry vinegar. The hot pepper flakes are my addition to the traditional recipe. Almonds and hazelnuts give extra dimension to this chunky, versatile sauce.

Makes about 2 cups

Uses: Romesco sauce is excellent on pasta or pizza and on its own as a dip for fresh bread and pita. Use it to give extra flavor to grilled fish, meat, and poultry or any kind of vegetable, grilled or fried.

1 large onion, halved (unpeeled)

1 whole head of garlic, halved crosswise

About 1 cup extra virgin olive oil

2 red bell peppers

4 or 5 large red unrefrigerated beefsteak tomatoes (about 3 pounds)

$1/4$ cup blanched almonds

$1/4$ cup hazelnuts

$1/2$ cup dried bread crumbs, preferably from sourdough, or more as needed

3 dried ñora peppers, soaked in warm water for 15 to 20 minutes

1 to 3 teaspoons Aleppo or Maraş pepper, or a pinch of hot red pepper flakes, to taste

1 tablespoon sherry vinegar, or to taste

1 teaspoon sea salt, or to taste

Preheat the oven to 450°F. Rub the onion halves and garlic with olive oil, place in a pan, and bake for 20 minutes.

Coat the bell peppers and tomatoes with olive oil and add to the pan with the half-baked onion. Bake for about 30 minutes, or until the onion, garlic, peppers, and tomatoes are soft.

Press the garlic to extract the baked cloves. Pass all the vegetables through a food mill fitted with the medium disk. Add the roasted garlic to the mill, and pass it through with the rest.

Warm 2 tablespoons of olive oil in a small skillet over medium heat and sauté the almonds and hazelnuts for 1 to 2 minutes, until golden. Add the bread crumbs, stir to coat with oil, and remove from the heat.

Drain the ñora peppers and place in a food processor with the almonds, bread crumbs, and Aleppo pepper. Process to a smooth paste.

Combine this mixture and the baked vegetables in a bowl and toss well. Add 5 tablespoons of olive oil, the vinegar, and the salt. You should have a thick, chunky sauce. If it looks thin, add more bread crumbs. Taste and adjust the seasoning.

Let the sauce cool, then pack in 2 half-pint jars, pressing well to avoid air pockets. Top with a thin film of olive oil, cover the jar and store in the refrigerator for about 3 weeks.

North African Pepper Sauce

Food writer Paula Wolfert, my mentor and an expert in North African and Mediterranean cooking, introduced me to homemade Tunisian harissa. It is so different from the commercial blend and quite easy to make. When I first tasted it during a visit to Tunisia, I immediately became addicted. It is incredible how just a small amount gives depth of flavor to salads—see the Tunisian Carrot Salad (page 87)—sauces, stews, and dressings. Since the flavorful Tunisian chile and all the North African chiles are hard to find, I offer two versions of harissa, one made with Mexican chiles and one with Italian peperoncini.

Uses: A little bowl of harissa mixed with fruity olive oil becomes an addictive dipping sauce for crusty bread. You can also spread the sauce on thin homemade bread dough (page 177) or on frozen pizza dough, topping it with fresh cheese and mushrooms or other vegetables to create a wonderful spicy focaccia. A little harissa enlivens salad dressing and marinades for meat, poultry, and fish.

Anissa's Harissa
MILD

This version was developed by my friend the well-known Lebanese food writer Anissa Helou. She makes a mild and flavorful harissa with dried guajillo and árbol chiles. Makes about 2 cups

9 ounces dried guajillo chiles

1 ounce dried chiles de árbol

$1/4$ cup caraway seeds

20 garlic cloves, peeled

Sea salt, to taste

Extra virgin olive oil to top the jars

Pull the stems off the chiles. Shake out and discard the seeds. Rinse the peppers under cold water, then soak them in boiling water for about 20 minutes.

Put the caraway seeds in a food processor and process for a minute or so. Add the garlic and a teaspoon of salt and process until the garlic is crushed.

Drain the chiles. Add to the garlic mixture with another teaspoon of salt, to taste—harissa needs to have enough salt without tasting salty. Process until you have a lightly textured paste. The chiles will not be completely mashed.

Taste, adding more salt if necessary. Spoon into 2 half-pint glass jars. Top with olive oil, which will keep the harissa from spoiling, and seal the jars. Make sure you add oil every time you spoon harissa out of the jar. Well covered in oil, harissa will keep for months in the refrigerator.

Harissa with Peperoncini and Aleppo Pepper

QUITE HOT

I make harissa with the peperoncini and Anaheim chiles I grow in my garden. I dry them to have on hand year-round. A combination of commercial dried Italian peperoncini and Aleppo is a good substitute. Makes about 2 cups

5 ounces whole dried peperoncini or a combination of peperoncini and Anaheim chiles

$1/4$ cup caraway seeds, coarsely ground in a mortar or food mill

5 ounces Aleppo pepper

15 garlic cloves, peeled

2 teaspoons sea salt, or more to taste

Extra virgin olive oil to top the jars

Remove the stems and some loose seeds before soaking the peperoncini in boiling water for about 30 minutes, then drain. Process the caraway, drained chiles, Aleppo pepper, and garlic in a blender or food processor, stopping and scraping the sides of the bowl with a spatula, until you have a coarse paste. Add salt and process for a few seconds.

Spoon into 2 half-pint glass jars. Top with olive oil and seal the jars. Make sure you add oil every time you spoon harissa out of the jar. Well covered in oil, harissa will keep for months in the refrigerator.

Hot Yemenite Sauce

Zhug was brought to Israel by Yemenite Jews and is now the hot condiment of choice in Israel. You will find zhug (which is also called *zhoug*) made with green or red chiles in falafel stands and in the kebab restaurants that serve *shawarma*—vertically skewered pieces of meat—accompanied by many different salads, spreads, relishes, and freshly baked pita bread. Zhug is made with fresh chiles, garlic, coriander, cardamom, and other spices. It is usually very hot, so you should start with a small amount. Mixed with soaked and ground fenugreek, it becomes *hilbeh*. I prefer to make my zhug with green chiles, to distinguish it from the other hot red sauces of the eastern Mediterranean.

Makes about 1 1/4 cups

Uses: You can add a little zhug to soups, pasta, and bean dishes, besides serving it as a condiment with Falafel (page 58) or slices of any fried vegetable. To make a delicious low-fat sauce or dip for vegetables, mix it with reduced or nonfat yogurt.

10 to 14 fresh jalapeño chiles, seeded and coarsely chopped

1 teaspoon sea salt

6 to 8 garlic cloves, coarsely chopped

1 teaspoon ground caraway seeds

1 teaspoon ground cumin seeds

1/2 teaspoon ground green cardamom

1 cup coarsely chopped fresh cilantro

1/2 cup packed fresh flat-leaf parsley leaves

1 teaspoon freshly ground black pepper

2 to 4 teaspoons fresh lemon juice

Put all the ingredients in a food processor or blender and pulse several times to make a smooth paste. You will have to scrape down all the bits and pieces that stick to the sides of the bowl. Pack in a 1-pint jar, screw on the lid, and store in the refrigerator. Zhug will keep for 1 to 2 weeks. You can also freeze it, but it will lose some of its garlicky flavor.

✦ All-Purpose Greek Tomato Sauce ✦

This is the sauce that I use for all kinds of dishes, from pasta to moussaka. The sweet wine balances the tartness of the tomatoes and together with the cinnamon gives the sauce depth of flavor. It freezes well, and I always make a few batches whenever fresh tomatoes are at their best (and have not lost their flavor due to refrigeration). Good-quality canned tomatoes are a good substitute in the winter.

Makes about 6 cups, enough for 2 pounds pasta

2/3 cup olive oil

2 cups finely chopped red onion

Sea salt

2 tablespoons tomato paste

1 1/2 cups sweet wine such as Marsala or Mavrodaphne, or more

2 to 3 teaspoons Aleppo or Maraş pepper, or a pinch of hot red pepper flakes, to taste

6 cups grated ripe fresh tomatoes (about 3 pounds; see page 212), or two 28-ounce cans diced tomatoes with their juice

Two 2 1/2-inch cinnamon sticks

Sugar or honey (optional)

Heat the olive oil in a medium saucepan over medium heat. Sprinkle the onion with salt and sauté, stirring often, for about 10 minutes, or until soft. Add the tomato paste and cook, stirring, for 2 minutes, or until glossy. Add the wine and pepper and simmer for 1 minute. Add the grated tomatoes, cinnamon sticks, salt to taste, and about 1 tablespoon sugar or honey if you like. Bring to a boil, reduce the heat to low, cover, and simmer for about 30 minutes or more, until the sauce thickens. Romove from the heat and discard the cinnamon sticks. Taste and add salt ot taste.

The sauce will keep in the refrigerator stored in non-reactive containers for up to 4 days. If you want to keep it longer, freeze it following the instructions for fresh tomato pulp on page 212.

✦ Mushroom, Olive, and Caper Sauce ✦ for Pasta

This sauce is best tossed with hot hollow pasta like penne or shells. Sprinkle with freshly chopped parsley or more rosemary and if desired with crumbled feta cheese. The pasta can then be eaten warm or at room temperature. I don't like cold pasta served directly from the refrigerator, as in most salad bars and take-out restaurants. It is convenient, however, to be able to cook pasta, drain it, then simply mix it with a flavorful cold sauce that you have made well in advance.

Makes about 3 cups, enough for 2 pounds pasta

Uses: Serve this sauce as an appetizer or a snack, spreading it over freshly toasted bread. You can also spread the sauce on thin homemade bread dough (page 177) or on frozen pizza dough to create a wonderful hearty focaccia. Besides pasta, the sauce can dress boiled potatoes, steamed cauliflower and broccoli, as well as grilled or boiled skinless chicken or turkey breast.

1 cup olive oil

$1^1/_2$ cups thinly sliced fresh mushrooms

1 to 3 small fresh chiles, preferably peperoncini, chopped

3 garlic cloves, chopped

$^1/_2$ cup dried porcini, soaked in 1 cup warm water for 30 minutes

$^1/_3$ cup plus 1 tablespoon sherry vinegar

2 tablespoons dry white wine

1 teaspoon dried Greek oregano, or 2 teaspoons fresh rosemary leaves

1 cup Kalamata olives, pitted (see page 213) and coarsely chopped

$^1/_2$ cup salt-packed capers, soaked in warm water, rinsed, and drained on paper towels

Sea salt and freshly ground black pepper

Warm 2 tablespoons of the olive oil in a medium skillet. Add the fresh mushrooms and sauté over high heat until soft, about 4 minutes. Add the chiles and garlic and sauté briefly, taking care not to let the garlic color. Drain the soaked porcini, saving the liquid. Chop and add to the pan with the liquid. Toss and remove from the heat.

Stir a couple of times and let cool a little, then add the vinegar and wine. Sprinkle with the oregano, transfer to a 1-quart jar, cover, and let stand overnight. Mix in the chopped olives, capers, and the remaining olive oil. Cover again, shake well, and taste. The sauce should have a robust flavor. Adjust the seasoning, but don't add salt if you plan to serve with feta.

Store in the refrigerator for up to 3 weeks. Remove from refrigerator at least 1 hour, and shake well, before serving.

Mushroom, Olive, and Caper Sauce for Pasta, page 23

Lemon, Honey, and Pepper Jelly, page 26

◆ Lemon, Honey, and Pepper Jelly ◆

I first prepared this jelly to preserve the abundant lemons from our two trees. I usually make lemon liqueur, thinly peeling the aromatic zest and macerating it in vodka. I julienne the leftover pith with some of the zest to make marmalade. Our lemons are not particularly juicy—we occasionally irrigate the lemon trees as our island gets little rain, even in the winter.

I find that I get more liquid out of the fruits by processing them in the blender than by juicing them, a technique that I think yields much more flavor even with regular juicy lemons.

If you want a perfectly clear jelly, pass the pulp through a strainer lined with cheesecloth. But I don't mind at all if my amber-colored jelly is cloudy; its flavor is wonderful. Makes about 3 cups

Uses: Serve this jelly with manouri, ricotta salata, mozzarella, or any creamy soft cheese, as well as with cold cuts and salami. I also use it as the base for vinaigrettes and various other hot and cold dressings. By adding garlic, olive oil, herbs, and more hot pepper, you can make a glaze for meat, poultry, mushrooms, and vegetables to be grilled.

4 or 5 lemons, preferably organic, washed and dried

2 cups mild honey, or a bit more

2 or 3 small dried hot chiles, halved lengthwise with scissors and seeds removed

Fresh rosemary sprigs (optional)

$2^1/2$ ounces liquid pectin, or 3 teaspoons agar-agar flakes (see Note)

Peel 4 lemons with a very sharp serrated knife, removing most of the white pith. You can, if you wish, julienne, blanch, and cook the peels in sugar or honey syrup to make marmalade. Or reserve for another use.

Over a bowl, quarter the lemons and remove the seeds and the white middle core, saving the juice. Put the lemon pieces and the juice from the bowl in a blender and process until you have a homogenous thick pulp. Pass through a medium-mesh strainer and measure it. If you don't have about 2 cups, peel and process one more lemon.

Bring the lemon pulp, honey, and chiles to a slow boil in a stainless-steel saucepan. Simmer for 3 minutes, turn up the heat, and cook, stirring, for another 3 minutes. Turn off the heat, add the rosemary sprigs if you're using it, cover, and let the mixture cool completely. You can set it aside overnight if you like. Taste and add more honey if you find it too sour, though it is supposed to be pleasantly tart and moderately hot, not sweet.

Discard the rosemary and bring again to a slow boil, add the pectin, and cook, stirring constantly, for 1 minute. Remove from the heat and continue to stir for another 2 minutes. If you are using agar-agar, sprinkle the flakes over the lemon-honey mixture and cook, stirring, for 5 to 6 minutes, until it thickens.

Remove the peppers if you wish and ladle the jelly into small jars. If you like, add a small fresh sprig of rosemary to each jar. Top each jelly with a circle of parchment paper, close the lids, and let cool. Stored in the fridge, it keeps for 3 months or more. If you want to keep it longer, cook in a water bath for 6 minutes to seal the jars.

Note
Agar-agar is a very powerful thickening agent extracted from seaweed. You can buy it at Asian groceries and health food stores.

◆ Olive, Almond, and Herb Spread ◆

This is my tapenade-like spread, which I always keep in the refrigerator. Authentic tapenade, the famous olive, caper, and anchovy spread of Provence, can be wonderful, but most of the jarred versions are so salty that all other flavors are lost. Both tapenade and pesto have their roots in antiquity. The Roman statesman Cato (234–149 B.C.) describes a preparation that combined pitted and chopped black, green, and mottled olives with coriander, fennel, cumin, rue, mint, olive oil, and vinegar. My olive spread is inspired by this ancient recipe.

Make the spread at least one day in advance to give the flavors a chance to meld. Serve with toasted bread as an appetizer. Makes about 2 cups

$1^1/2$ cups juicy black olives

$1^1/2$ cups cracked green Greek olives (Nafplion)

3 tablespoons chopped fresh cilantro

$1/2$ cup chopped fresh wild fennel or cultivated fennel fronds plus 1 teaspoon ground fennel seeds

2 garlic cloves, peeled

$2/3$ cup unsalted almonds, preferably with skins

3 tablespoons chopped fresh mint leaves

2 or 3 canned jalapeño chiles and/or freshly ground white pepper to taste

$1^1/2$ tablespoons red wine vinegar

1 to 2 tablespoons balsamic vinegar, or to taste

$1/4$ cup plus 1 tablespoon extra virgin olive oil

Olive oil to top the jar

Rinse the olives in running water. Taste them, and if they are still very salty, let them stand for 1 to 2 hours in lukewarm water before rinsing again. Dry on paper towels. Remove the pits (see page 213).

Place the olives, cilantro, fennel, fennel seeds, if using, garlic, almonds, mint, jalapeños, red wine vinegar, and 1 tablespoon of the balsamic vinegar in a food processor. Process until you get a smooth paste, then, with the motor running, slowly add the extra virgin olive oil. Taste and adjust the seasoning, adding a little white pepper or more balsamic vinegar if needed.

Transfer the olive paste to a jar, top with a little olive oil so that the paste is completely covered, cover the jar, and place in the refrigerator for at least 1 day before serving. The spread will keep for up to 4 weeks in the refrigerator.

Onion, Hot Pepper, and Turmeric Paste

A specialty of southern Tunisia, *hrous* is made with onions instead of the garlic in harissa and also has more spices. In the traditional recipe for this flavorful paste, large quantities of onions are sprinkled with salt and turmeric and left to ferment in clay jars for about three months before the chiles and spices are mixed in. This simpler version is based on Paula Wolfert's recipe, from her marvelous book *The Cooking of the Eastern Mediterranean.* Makes about 2 cups

Uses: Hrous flavors all kinds of couscous dishes and can deepen the flavor of any meat, poultry, or vegetable stew. I also like to add hrous to my basic tomato sauce. See Harissa (page 19) for more ideas.

2 pounds onions, thickly sliced

$1/3$ to $1/2$ cup coarse sea salt

1 tablespoon ground turmeric

20 dried New Mexican chiles

10 dried chipotle chiles

1 tablespoon plus 2 teaspoons coriander seeds

$1/4$ cup plus 1 tablespoon caraway seeds

2 to 3 tablespoons dried rosebuds (optional)

1 teaspoon ground cinnamon

Olive oil

Toss the onions with the salt and turmeric in a large bowl. Let stand for about 3 days, tossing every now and then, until the onions become very soft. Transfer the onions to a strainer lined with cheesecloth and let them drain. Gather the ends of the cloth and squeeze the onions to extract all their liquid. It is easier to fully drain the onions in 2 to 3 batches.

Cut off the stems and discard the seeds of the dried chiles. In a blender, spice grinder, or clean coffee grinder, grind the chiles in batches, with the coriander, caraway, and rosebuds if you're using them. Be careful as you do this to avoid irritating your nose and eyes with the peppery fumes.

Combine the spice mixture, drained onions, cinnamon, and $1/4$ cup plus 1 tablespoon olive oil. Wearing rubber gloves, knead to mix well. Pack into a jar and top with more olive oil. Hrous will keep for about 4 months in the refrigerator.

✦ Mixed Herb and Chile Paste ✦

Although we can find quite decent fresh herbs all year, that wasn't always the case. Many years ago, watching a French TV cooking show, I came upon an ingenious flavor-packed herb paste. The guest chef, whose name unfortunately I don't remember, spoke about the herbs in salt his grandmother kept in a jar by her stove. In the winter, when her garden was frozen, she used a teaspoon of herb paste to flavor soups and sauces. The chef said that he continued the tradition and always kept a jar of mixed herbs in his professional kitchen. He explained that he used the best and freshest spring herbs he got at the farmers' market or from his friends' gardens, assuring the audience that his paste was more flavorful than freshly chopped supermarket herbs. Once I tried it, I was absolutely convinced he was right. I have altered the original recipe to suit my taste, adding either wild fennel or dill and always fresh hot chile, besides parsley. Note that the mixture is very salty, so it is unlikely that you will need to add more salt to any dish that you flavor with it.

You will need kitchen scales to measure the ingredients for this recipe. The mixture may spoil fast if the measurements are not exact. Makes about 2 cups

Uses: Add about 1 tablespoon to every quart of soup (such as chicken, vegetable, or bean) and $^1/2$ to 1 teaspoon to sauces made with meat or poultry stock.

3 ounces fresh flat-leaf parsley leaves, most stems cut off, washed and dried

3 ounces fresh celery leaves, most stems cut off, or fresh dill and/or fennel tops, washed and dried

5 ounces leeks, white part only, washed and sliced

1 ounce fresh chiles, seeded

$2^1/2$ ounces sea salt

Place the herbs, leeks, and chiles in a food processor and process, starting and stopping the motor, to make a paste. Transfer the mixture to a nonreactive bowl, add the salt, and mix very well. Pack into a 1-pint glass jar and cover. The paste will keep for up to 1 year in the refrigerator.

✦ Anchovy and Peperoncino Olive Oil ✦

This is a spicy Italian version of *nam pla*—the omnipresent Asian fish sauce. Contrary to what you might think, it is not a made-up concoction. *Garum* or *liquamen* was the favorite sauce of both the ancient Greeks and Romans—as ubiquitous in those days as ketchup is today. It was made from small fish and fish guts that were left to ferment in the sun with salt, vinegar, and spices. This strong sauce was used to flavor all kinds of foods, including vegetables, dried beans, meat, and fish. The various Italian anchovy sauces, like the *Colatura di alici* from Cetara (see Sources), is a modern version of the ancient *liquamen*, as is the old English standby Worcestershire sauce. Use more or fewer anchovies, to suit your taste; just be sure they are the best quality. Makes about 2 cups

Uses: This is a wonderful dressing for tomato salad and grilled or steamed vegetables. It is particularly good with cauliflower and broccoli. With the addition of garlic and herbs it becomes an ideal sauce for pasta (see Pasta con le Sarde, page 166).

5 to 10 good-quality anchovy fillets in olive oil, drained on paper towels

2 cups extra virgin olive oil

2 to 4 dried peperoncini (or any other chile), halved lengthwise with scissors but left attached at the stem

Chop 3 or 4 of the anchovies and place in a stainless-steel saucepan over low heat. Add 1 cup of the olive oil and 2 or more peperoncini, according to your taste. When the oil is quite warm to the touch, remove it from the heat. Let cool and transfer to a clean and absolutely dry 2-cup bottle. Add the whole anchovies to taste and more chiles if you like and fill the bottle with the rest of the olive oil. Cap and let stand in a dark place for 2 to 3 days, shaking from time to time, before using. Stored in a cool, dark place, this oil will keep for about 3 months.

✦ Figs in Spicy Sweet-and-Sour Marinade ✦

All kinds of fresh or dried fruits—especially peaches, apricots, pears, prunes, and plums—can be macerated in a combination of vinegar and sugar or honey. The sweet-and-sour fruits traditionally accompany duck and rabbit, but also pork and lamb in Provence, the Mediterranean coast of France. The bay leaves give the dish a Greek touch. Greeks always use bay leaves when they cook figs. You can marinate prunes, dried apricots, peaches, and sultanas in the same spicy sweet-and-sour mixture. Makes 2 cups

Uses: Serve with thinly sliced prosciutto, bresaola, and smoked ham or with rabbit, game, roasted chicken, turkey, or duck. I also like to pair these figs with soft creamy cheeses like ricotta, manouri, and fresh goat's cheese served on a board or in sandwiches.

3/4 pound good-quality dried figs, preferably imported Greek or Turkish or a combination of Californian and Mediterranean

1 teaspoon whole cloves

2 Turkish bay leaves

2 small mild dried chiles, or more to taste

One 2-inch cinnamon stick

About 1 cup sherry vinegar or other good-quality wine vinegar

2 to 3 tablespoons honey

Pack the figs into a sterilized 1-pint glass jar. Add the cloves, bay leaves, chiles, and cinnamon stick.

In a nonreactive saucepan, warm the vinegar with the honey over low heat and stir until the honey dissolves, being careful not to let the mixture boil. Pour the warm vinegar-honey mixture over the figs, topping with a little more vinegar if needed to cover the figs completely. Close the jar and leave in a cool place for at least 1 week before using, shaking from time to time. The figs will keep for a year or more. As you consume them, you can add more figs to the honey-vinegar mixture in the jar.

✦ Lemon Slices in Spicy Olive Oil ✦

Westerners tend to use just the juice of the lemon, but North Africans preserve whole lemons in a brine made with lemon juice and plenty of coarse sea salt. They eat the skin and white pith of the preserved lemons, which acquire a distinctive flavor and aroma. Chop and add to potato salads, steamed cauliflower, carrots, broccoli, or bitter greens; also to grilled chicken or fish, and to stuffings for pork and poultry, and wherever "preserved lemons" are called for. Besides the slices, use a few drops of the strongly flavored olive oil, to which you may add a few chiles, to enliven dressings and marinades. Makes 2 cups

3 or 4 lemons, preferably organic

4 to 6 tablespoons sea salt

2 to 3 dried peperoncini (or any other chile), cut in half lengthwise with scissors but still attached to the stem

About 1 cup olive oil

Wash and dry the lemons thoroughly. Cut them into $1/8$-inch-thick slices and lay one layer in a stainless-steel colander. Sprinkle the lemon slices with plenty of salt and repeat, making more layers until you have used all the lemons and salt. Set aside to drain for 24 hours.

Press the lemon slices carefully with paper towels to extract most of the juice, then pack the slices in a 1-pint jar, adding the peperoncini between the slices. Completely cover the lemon slices with olive oil. Close the jar. The lemon slices will keep in the refrigerator for 3 to 6 months.

Figs in Spicy Sweet-and-Sour Marinade, page 32

Lemon Slices in Spicy Olive Oil, page 33

Chiles Preserved in Olive Oil

The small Italian *peperoncini* belong to the same family as the cayenne and the fiery Indian chiles (*Capsicum frutescens,* also known as bird's-eye or Tabasco peppers). In the open-air vegetable markets throughout Italy during autumn you will find crates full of entire peperoncini plants, with their bright red fruits standing up like candles. Besides being deliciously hot and fragrant, they are so beautiful that you'll feel like putting them in a vase. The great thing about peperoncini is that they are easy to grow, even in pots, and make a perfect addition to any summer flower and herb patch.

This recipe is a great way to preserve the fresh chiles of the garden or the ones you get from the farmers' market. There is no way to give you exact proportions as they depend on the kind and size of the chiles you choose to preserve. But the method applies to all. The recipe is my variation from Patience Gray's unsur-passed book Honey from a Weed. "The oil can be used with or without 1 or 2 hot peppers to enliven many a winter dish," Mrs. Gray suggests, and I couldn't agree more.

Uses: Peperoncini sott'Olio can be served as a meze, with ouzo or raki. Chop and add to salads and spreads, or to mizithra, feta, or any spreadable cheese to create a topping for toasted bruschette. Drops of the spicy olive oil can be added to dressings for raw or steamed vegetable salads, and to soups.

Small or medium vine-ripened peperoncini, Anaheim, guajillo, New Mexican, or other fresh red chiles

Sea salt

Fresh rosemary sprigs or dried Turkish bay leaves (optional)

Olive oil

Wearing rubber gloves, use scissors to cut a slit in the calyx (the green cup around the stem) of each chile to expose the seeds. Sprinkle with salt, making sure that some grains reach the inside of the pepper. Let the chiles rest in a colander for about 24 hours to wilt.

Wearing rubber gloves, press them on paper towels to extract the juices and extra salt. Pack them in jars and add a sprig of rosemary or a bay leaf if you like. Cover with olive oil and top with a piece of parchment paper to make sure the chiles are fully submerged. Close the lids and shake every now and then for about a week before using.

If you make large quantities and you want to keep them for a long time, process the filled jars in a water bath, boiling for 5 to 10 minutes, depending on the size of the jar. You can also store the jars in the refrigerator, but the oil will solidify, and you will have to let the chiles and oil come to room temperature before using.

Small Eggplants Stuffed with Chile, Garlic, and Parsley

Pickled stuffed eggplants are sold in jars all over the Mediterranean but are usually very sour. In this recipe, my mother's adaptation, the eggplants are steamed or blanched, stuffed, and then drizzled with a vinaigrette. The resulting appetizer has a smoother and sweeter taste, which is spiked by the pungent garlic-chile filling.

Serves 10 to 12 as an appetizer

Uses: Serve as an appetizer or as part of a meze spread. Great as an accompaniment to grilled fish, poultry, or meat. Paired with mozzarella, ricotta, manouri, or fresh goat cheese, they make great bruschette and sandwiches.

24 small eggplants, each about 3 inches long (about 2 pounds)

Coarse sea salt

2 cups chopped fresh flat-leaf parsley, mostly leaves

3 or 4 garlic cloves, chopped

3 to 6 jalapeño or other fresh green chiles, seeded and finely chopped

VINAIGRETTE

$1/3$ cup good-quality red wine vinegar or sherry vinegar

3 tablespoons balsamic vinegar

2 tablespoons fresh lemon juice

$1/2$ cup extra virgin olive oil

Cut the stem from each eggplant and wash and dry them. Make a slash lengthwise, starting $1/3$ inch from the stem and finishing $1/3$ inch from the tip of each eggplant. Sprinkle a fair amount of salt inside the cut. Let the eggplants stand for about 1 hour. Rinse under cold water and pat dry with paper towels. Arrange in a steamer and steam, tossing once, for 20 minutes or more, until tender when pierced with a fork. Or blanch the eggplants in 1 gallon boiling water, without rinsing away the salt. Drain for several hours in a colander, then let dry overnight on paper towels.

Mix the parsley, garlic, and chiles with 1 to 2 teaspoons salt in a bowl. Toss well with your fingers to wilt the parsley. Place the drained eggplants in a glass or clay dish that holds them in one layer. Stuff the slash in each eggplant with the parsley mixture.

Whisk together the vinegars, lemon juice, and olive oil and pour over the stuffed eggplants. Cover and refrigerate for at least 1 day before serving. The eggplants keep refrigerated for about 3 weeks. Let come to room temperature before serving.

⋅ Pink Cauliflower and Turnip Pickles ⋅

These brightly colored pickles are as lovely to look at as they are delicious to eat. Beets are used throughout the Middle East and North Africa to color the vegetables.

Makes about 2 quarts

Uses: The cauliflower florets and the sliced turnips or radishes are served on their own, as a meze that accompanies the strong anise-flavored raki or ouzo, but they can also be added to salads, like the macerated cabbage and carrot Missir (page 83). Serve as you would pickled cucumbers, as an accompaniment to cold meat and cheese sandwiches.

1 pound turnips or a combination of turnips and radishes

1 pound cauliflower

4 to 5 cups white wine vinegar

$1/4$ cup sugar, or to taste

3 small red beets, diced

2 fresh jalapeño chiles

2 Turkish bay leaves

2 tablespoons coriander seeds

Peel the turnips. Cut the turnips (and radishes if you're using them) into $1/4$-inch-thick slices and cut the cauliflower into small florets.

Warm 2 cups of the vinegar with the sugar in a nonreactive saucepan over medium heat until the sugar dissolves. Use more or less sugar according to how acidic you like your pickles, bearing in mind that traditionally Mediterranean pickles are much more sour than American pickles.

Pack the turnips, radishes, and cauliflower into two 1-quart jars. Divide the diced beets, the chiles, bay leaves, coriander, and warm vinegar-sugar mixture between the jars. Top with more vinegar as needed to cover the vegetables completely. Seal and keep in a cool, dark place. Shake from time to time for the first 3 days. The pickles will be ready to eat after 4 to 5 days and will keep well for 3 months or more in a cool, dark place.

✦ Olives in Harissa, Garlic, ✦ and Orange-Lemon Dressing

Olives are an essential part of the Mediterranean table. Many people still cure their own (see Note), but most choose from the very wide variety of jarred olives available in supermarkets and specialty stores. Kalamata and a few other olives can be eaten right out of the jar, but most olives sold in brine need to be drained and then dressed before being served. Often a simple dressing of just a little olive oil and a sprinkling of fresh herbs (oregano, rosemary, thyme) is enough. This is a more elaborate dressing, inspired by the olives I tasted in a Lebanese restaurant in Athens. Slightly bitter Seville orange juice, garlic, harissa, and olive oil make an ideal dressing for green as well as firm black olives. Unfortunately, Seville oranges are not widely available, so you can use a combination of orange and lemon juice. Makes 3 cups

14 ounces Greek green olives (Nafplion), or a combination of various excellent-quality green, brown, and firm black olives

2 teaspoons Harissa (page 19)

1/4 cup fresh lemon juice

2 tablespoons fresh orange juice

1 cup extra virgin olive oil, or more as needed

Zest of 1 orange, cut into strips

2 garlic cloves, quartered lengthwise

1 tablespoon fresh rosemary leaves

Wash the olives thoroughly under running water. Drain them well in a colander and press dry on paper towels.

Mix the harissa with the lemon and orange juices in a bowl. Add the olive oil and whisk well. Pack the olives in layers in a 3-cup jar, placing orange zest and pieces of garlic between layers of olives. Pour the olive oil mixture over them. If the olives are not completely covered, top with a little more olive oil. Seal and set aside at room temperature for 1 to 2 days. Store in the refrigerator. One hour before serving, take out as many as you need and let stand at room temperature. The olives will keep in the refrigerator for up to 1 month.

Note

If you can get ripe, freshly harvested (black) olives in late fall, place them in a basket or colander set over a bucket or a large bowl. Sprinkle generously with coarse sea salt and let them stand for 6 to 8 days, tossing twice a day. When their flesh turns black all the way to the kernel, rinse them briefly with running water, drain, and let them dry on paper towels overnight. Then sauté (see page 62), or keep in the spicy dressing described here.

◆ Pickled Octopus ◆

Pickled octopus is one of the most common Greek mezedes, served with ouzo in taverns all over the country. In the souks of Tunisia dried octopus is sold, along with small dried fish, like smelt and tiny shrimp. All these dried sea creatures are soaked in water and added to fish couscous and other dishes.

To serve pickled octopus, drain one or two tentacles, slice them, and dress with extra virgin olive oil, sprinkling with fresh or dried savory or oregano.

Makes $1^1/2$ quarts, serving 12 or more as an appetizer

4 Turkish bay leaves

1 octopus (about 2 pounds), cleaned

3 to $3^1/2$ cups good-quality red wine vinegar

1 tablespoon honey

3 or 4 garlic cloves, halved lengthwise

3 or 4 dried peperoncini or other small chiles, halved lengthwise with scissors but left attached at the stem

2 tablespoons coriander seeds

2 or 3 fresh thyme or savory sprigs

Olive oil to top the jar

Bring 2 quarts water to a boil with 1 bay leaf in a large pot. With tongs, or wearing a silicone glove, hold the octopus head and submerge briefly (3 to 5 seconds) in the water three times. The technique is supposed to keep the tentacles straight, and it usually works. Finally, let the octopus cook in the water for 15 minutes, until firm and easily pierced with a fork. It shouldn't be tender, because it will get too mushy in the vinegar brine.

In a nonreactive saucepan, bring the vinegar, honey, garlic, chiles, and coriander to a boil and immediately remove from the heat.

Drain the octopus and separate the tentacles with a sharp knife. Place the cut-up octopus in a $1^1/2$-quart jar with the remaining bay leaves and the sprigs of thyme or savory. Pour the warm vinegar with the chiles, garlic, and other ingredients over the octopus to cover it completely. Add 1 inch of olive oil at the top. Cover and keep at room temperature, shaking every now and then. It will be ready to serve after 1 week and will keep for 1 or 2 months in the refrigerator. Bring the pieces you want to serve to room temperature.

Homemade Bulgur, Milk, and Yogurt Pasta

There is an ongoing dispute over the origin of this unique Balkan and eastern Mediterranean staple. Some scholars claim that trahana can be traced back to Persia (Iran) or even to the steppes of China. The Ottomans spread trahana to the West, they say, through their vast empire. Other scholars, citing the ancient word *tracta,* insist that trahana was a Greek "pasta" that spread eastward. Interestingly enough, in some parts of Greece the crumblike pasta made with cracked wheat, milk, and yogurt is called *ksinohondros—ksino* meaning "sour" and *hondros* "coarsely ground wheat" in ancient Greek. Whatever the name and origin, this pasta is the perfect way to preserve the grains and surplus milk of early summer, combining them to produce a rich and nourishing staple for the winter months. Trahana might have been invented by various people in different parts of the world.

I wouldn't have suggested that you make trahana from scratch if there were a decent commercial alternative. Unfortunately, there isn't. The packages labeled *trahana* have nothing to do with the real thing, and if you don't want to make it, it is better to use the substitutes I suggest in the recipes. The process may seem long, but the actual work, the cooking of the grain, takes less than thirty minutes as bulgur cooks much faster than the original cracked wheat our ancestors used. The pasta must dry completely, spread in the sun for a few days, as was the custom. Today you can dry it in a dehydrator or in a very low oven.

Following the old island tradition, I use barley flour together with the bulgur. In some parts of the Mediterranean trahana was made entirely from barley instead of cracked wheat. Barley used to be the staple grain of the islands, grown on small terraced arid and windy pieces of land, where wheat couldn't be cultivated. Makes about 1 pound

Uses: Trahana is most often made into soup (recipe follows). Trahana is also used instead of rice in vegetable stuffings, in meatballs, and in stews with or without meat.

1 quart whole milk, preferably sheep's or goat's

3 cups yogurt, preferably sheep's milk (not thick)

1 teaspoon sea salt

3 tablespoons Aleppo or Maraş pepper, or a pinch of hot red pepper flakes, to taste (optional)

$2^1/2$ cups medium bulgur

1 cup whole barley flour (see Sources) or fine semolina

3 to 4 tablespoons fresh lemon juice

In a pot, stir together the milk, yogurt, salt, and pepper if you're using it. Heat over medium heat until very warm. Whisking steadily, add the bulgur and barley flour or semolina and lemon juice. Continue to whisk constantly. When the mixture starts to boil, lower the heat and simmer, stirring, for about 10 minutes or more, until very thick. Remove from the heat and continue stirring for a few more minutes to prevent it from sticking to the bottom of the pot.

Line 2 baking sheets with parchment paper, and with a ladle transfer about $^1/2$-cup portions of the mixture to the baking sheets, flattening them with a spatula and leaving about $^1/2$ inch space between them. You may need more than 2 pans.

Let cool completely. The pieces will become like wet crumbly biscuits. Invert the pieces, breaking them into crumbs, and spread them on the sheets. Preheat the oven to its lowest temperature (about 150°F).

Place the baking sheets in the oven and let the crumbs dry, changing the position of the sheets and tossing the pieces with spatulas every now and then for about 4 hours. Turn the heat off and slightly open the oven door—put a wooden spoon at the opening, leaving the sheets with the trahana to cool completely overnight.

The next day, close the door and heat the oven to 150°F. Continue drying the trahana, changing the position of the sheets and tossing the crumbs every now and then for about 12 hours or more, until bone-dry and very hard.

Or dry the trahana crumbs in a dehydrator at 100° to 115°F, for about 3 days. Let cool completely and store in airtight jars. Properly dried trahana keeps for years, like dried pasta.

⋆ Trahana Soup ⋆

Fried bread crumbs often accompany this soup. Makes 4 servings

5 to 6 cups chicken, fish, or vegetable stock

2 to 3 cups chopped fresh or canned tomatoes (optional)

$^1/_2$ to $^2/_3$ cup trahana crumbs (preceding recipe)

Extra virgin olive oil

Aleppo pepper

Feta cheese, crumbled

Bring the stock to a boil in a saucepan with the tomato if you're using it. Add the trahana crumbs and simmer for about 20 minutes, stirring now and then, until the trahana is tender and thickens to a creamy consistency. To serve, drizzle olive oil on top of each bowl, sprinkle with pepper, and scatter on crumbled feta.

MEZEDES,
APPETIZERS,
and SALADS

"The cook sets before you a large tray on which are five small plates. One of these holds garlic, another a pair of sea-urchins, another a sweet wine sop, another ten cockles, the last a small piece of sturgeon. While I'm eating this, another is eating that; and while he is eating that, I have made away with this. What I want, good sir, is both the one and the other, but my wish is impossible. For I have neither five mouths nor five hands. . . ."

This quote, from an ancient comedy, written in the fourth to third century B.C., describes the frustration some people feel when they fail to taste all the dishes of a meze spread.

MEZEDES, TAPAS, AND ANTIPASTI ARE TRADITIONALLY SERVED IN the middle of the table, for people to share. Mediterranean meals often start—and sometimes end—with an array of small dishes that are savored leisurely, while sipping wine or the strong anise-flavored ouzo or raki.

A meze spread may include bean, vegetable, and cheese spreads; fried or marinated seafood; salads of raw, grilled, or steamed vegetables; sometimes fried meatballs or lamb's innards. A couple of tablespoons from a leftover stew on a piece of bread, some olives, pickled peppers or other vegetables, a piece of cheese, a slice of tomato with an anchovy and other canned or home-cured fish and meat can also be mezedes. These nibbles are great for stand-up parties, or to accompany drinks, or they may be combined and served in groups or one after the other to make a full meal.

It is not easy to prepare a meze lunch or dinner. The cook needs to be well organized and use pantry items and half-cooked ingredients creatively as building blocks for the many small plates needed for a full meze spread (see "Do-Ahead Spice Blends, Sauces, and Condiments," page 10). When I have to feed a crowd with various little dishes, I rely on my home-baked breads and savory biscotti (see page 177), which I always have on hand. I also keep a piece of my dough in the freezer, to whip up a flat bread with some topping—fresh or cured sardines and anchovies, chile oil, and a handful of garden herbs. Slices of fresh or toasted homemade bread accompany an olive and herb spread (page 28), Tyrokafteri (page 55), or a densely flavored Caponata (page 67), all dishes prepared well ahead of time and kept in the refrigerator for days.

Bear in mind that there is no clear distinction between mezedes and main courses, and a few of the dishes in this category could well be served as accompaniments to fish or meat or even as a main course themselves. The salads and the two cold soups are classic appetizers, though, even by the strictest rules of the classic Western food tradition.

I would like to start with four of my favorite mezedes/snacks. They are nonrecipes, and only the fried potatoes involve real cooking. The rest can be assembled in just minutes, even by a child.

- Toasted bread or whole wheat pita, drizzled with olive oil and sprinkled with fragrant Za'atar (page 14) or nutty Dukkah (page 15).

- Slices of *avgotaraho* (Greek botargo) drizzled with extra virgin olive oil and served with toasted whole wheat bread and lemon twists. Often called "Greek caviar," avgotaraho is the pressed and smoked eggs of gray mullet. It is considered the utmost delicacy in Greece, served on special occasions. Zaytinya (José Andrés's renowned eastern Mediterranean restaurant in Washington, D.C.) introduced it to the American public.

- Toast slices of chewy whole wheat bread, like my Basic Bread with Spices (page 177) and brush with fruity extra virgin olive oil while still warm. Sprinkle with Aleppo or Maraş pepper and top with shavings of good-quality bitter chocolate.

- Cut medium-small potatoes into about $1/8$-inch-thick slices on a mandoline and fry in olive oil in a skillet. Sprinkle lightly with salt and crumbled dried Greek oregano and serve with yogurt-feta dip on the side. I use $1/2$ cup crumbled feta mixed with 1 cup yogurt and 2 teaspoons Aleppo or Maraş pepper.

Sweet-and-Sour Eggplants with Nuts, Sultanas, Basil, and Peperoncino

I love these sweet-and-sour Calabrian eggplants, which are crunchy with nuts and fragrant with basil and mint. They are great as a side dish with any cold meat, grilled lamb chops, or chicken legs. Traditionally, though, they are an antipasto (appetizer) served on the sideboard. They also make a wonderful bruschetta spread on toasted bread with shavings of Parmesan, thin slices of mozzarella, manouri, or ricotta salata, or sprinkled with crumbled feta. Makes 6 to 8 servings as an appetizer

Sea salt

2 or 3 eggplants (about 2 pounds), cut into 1-inch cubes

3 to 4 tablespoons olive oil

SAUCE

4 garlic cloves, minced, or more to taste

2 tablespoons coarsely chopped almonds

$1/2$ cup coarsely chopped walnuts

8 to 10 fresh basil leaves

5 or 6 fresh mint leaves

$1/2$ cup good-quality red wine vinegar

2 teaspoons honey, or to taste

2 or 3 good pinches of chopped dried peperoncini or Aleppo or Maraş pepper, or a pinch of hot red pepper flakes, to taste

3 tablespoons sultanas (golden raisins)

Generously salt the eggplants, toss, and let drain in a colander for 1 hour, tossing once. Rinse under cold running water and pat dry with paper towels. Preheat the broiler. Line a baking sheet with parchment paper and place the eggplant cubes on it in a single layer. Drizzle with the olive oil, toss, and set the baking sheet about 5 inches from the heat source. Broil, tossing twice, until golden, 10 to 15 minutes. (You may need to do this in batches.) Or you can stir-fry the eggplant cubes in olive oil, then drain on paper towels.

Transfer the eggplant cubes to a large bowl and add the garlic, salt to taste, the almonds, and the walnuts. Tear the basil and mint leaves into pieces with your fingers or cut with scissors and add to the eggplant, tossing briefly.

Warm the vinegar and honey in a saucepan over low heat, stirring just to mix. Remove from the heat and add the peperoncini and sultanas. Pour over the eggplant while still hot. Toss and add more salt or pepper to taste. Let cool, cover, and refrigerate at least overnight and preferably for a day. Bring to room temperature before serving.

Garlic, Potato, Almond, and Yogurt Sauce

Each Mediterranean country has its version of garlic sauce: the Spanish *allioli*, the Turkish and Middle Eastern *tarator*, and the French *aïoli*, to name a few. The spicy brick-colored aïoli of Provence is spiked with the wonderful piment d'Espelette (see page 6) and is a garlicky fresh egg mayonnaise. Most other Mediterranean garlic sauces, though, use as a base a handful of soaked stale bread, mashed potatoes, and/or finely ground almonds or walnuts. This is my adaptation of my friend Vali Manouelides's *skordalia,* one of the best I have tasted—and I have tasted hundreds. Makes about 4 cups

Uses: Serve as a dip or spread with crusty fresh or toasted bread slices or with raw vegetables. Traditionally skordalia accompanies fried mussels, grilled or fried fish, batter-fried eggplant and zucchini slices, stuffed grape leaves, and steamed broccoli, cauliflower, beets, and green beans.

8 to 12 large garlic cloves, peeled

$1^1/2$ teaspoons sea salt

1 cup blanched almonds, soaked in water for about 3 hours and drained

2 tablespoons white wine vinegar, or more to taste

1 cup country bread, crusts removed, soaked in water, and squeezed dry

1 cup mashed potato

1 to 2 teaspoons piment d'Espelette, Aleppo pepper, or Maraş pepper, or a good pinch of cayenne, to taste

$1/2$ cup light olive oil or sunflower oil

$1/2$ cup extra virgin olive oil

1 cup Greek yogurt, preferably sheep's milk (see page 213)

1 teaspoon finely grated lemon zest

1 teaspoon sumac (optional)

Put the garlic, salt, almonds, and vinegar in a food processor and process to a sandlike mixture. Add the bread, potato, and pepper and process briefly. With the motor running, slowly pour in the light olive oil and then the extra virgin until you have a thick creamy paste.

Transfer to a bowl, cover, and refrigerate for a few hours or overnight. It keeps for 2 to 3 weeks in the refrigerator. Just before serving, stir in the yogurt and lemon zest. Taste and adjust the seasoning. Sprinkle with sumac if you like and serve.

Garlic, Lemon, and Walnut Sauce

This is a somewhat milder and certainly more digestible version of the classic Greek skordalia and the Middle Eastern tarator, both of which are traditionally prepared with stronger-tasting raw garlic cloves. The Greek Michelin-starred chef Lefteris Lazarou insists on using only roasted garlic in all the wonderful dishes he creates in his acclaimed Varoulko restaurant. He inspired me to come up with this deep-flavored yet light and mildly hot skordalia. Even people who normally avoid garlic can enjoy this spread.

Makes about $2^1/2$ cups

Uses: Skordalia can be spread on toasted bread or served with crudités. It can also be used as a dressing for sautéed, steamed, or grilled fish or vegetables. It is especially good with beets and steamed potatoes. If too thick, stir in 1 or 2 tablespoons white wine to make it pourable.

2 heads of garlic (see Note)

$1/2$ cup plus 2 teaspoons olive oil, preferably extra virgin

Sea salt

1 thick slice good-quality white bread, crusts removed, soaked in water, and squeezed dry (about $1/2$ cup)

$1/2$ cup mashed potato

1 teaspoon or more Aleppo or Maraş pepper, or a pinch of hot red pepper flakes, to taste

$1/2$ cup chopped walnuts

2 tablespoons lightly toasted pine nuts (see page 213)

$1/3$ to $1/2$ cup fresh lemon juice

Preheat the oven to 350°F.

Cut about $3/4$ inch off the top of each head of garlic and pour about a teaspoon of olive oil over the exposed flesh. Sprinkle with some salt, wrap in aluminum foil, and bake for 1 hour or more, until very soft. Open the foil and let the garlic cool a bit. Squeeze the garlic flesh out of the husks into a food processor.

Add the bread, potato, pepper, and nuts to the roasted garlic. Pour in 3 tablespoons of the lemon juice and process until the mixture is smooth. Gradually, with the motor running, add the remaining olive oil. Taste and add more lemon juice, salt, or pepper to taste. The skordalia keeps for up to 2 weeks in the refrigerator.

Note

Instead of roasting just 2 heads of garlic, you can roast a dozen. Mash the flesh to make a paste, adding more salt, and keep in jars topped with olive oil. Roasted garlic paste keeps for about 3 months in the refrigerator.

✦ Eggplant, Pepper, and Parsley Spread ✦

In some Greek and Middle Eastern taverns this smoky grilled eggplant spread is served inside the charred skin of the eggplant. I find it quite difficult to grill the eggplants so that the skins are well blackened but still firm enough to hold a filling, but give it a try if you like. Whichever way you present it, the flavor of this spread is deep and addictive. You can even lighten it, adding a couple of tablespoons of thick yogurt just before serving.

Serve as an appetizer with toasted bread or crudités. It is also good on baked or steamed potatoes and on steamed or grilled fillets of fish, as well as with chicken breast.

Makes about 3^1/2 cups, serving 8 to 10 as an appetizer

2 or 3 large eggplants (about 2 pounds)

3 tablespoons olive oil

3 large green bell peppers, halved and cut into ^{1}/2-inch pieces

1 or 2 jalapeño chiles, coarsely chopped

1 teaspoon Aleppo or Maraş pepper, or a pinch of hot red pepper flakes, to taste

1 or 2 garlic cloves, peeled and halved

1^1/2 cups fresh flat-leaf parsley leaves

^{1}/2 cup almonds

2 teaspoons sherry vinegar, or to taste

^{1}/4 cup extra virgin olive oil

Sea salt

1 teaspoon sumac (optional)

Preheat the broiler.

Broil the whole eggplants close to the heat source, turning occasionally, until the skins blacken on all sides, about 40 minutes total, to develop a smoky flavor. For an even smokier flavor, grill on the barbecue or over a gas flame. If you have an electric stove, place 3 layers of aluminum foil on a burner, place the eggplants on the foil, and let the skin blacken on 1 or 2 sides before you turn the eggplants to cook on all sides until soft, 20 to 30 minutes total.

When they are cool enough to handle, peel the eggplants and discard any large seeds. Drain in a colander, pressing to extract the juices.

Warm the 3 tablespoons olive oil in a skillet over medium-high heat. Sauté the green peppers and jalapeños, stirring often, until soft, about 10 minutes. Add the Aleppo pepper, remove from the heat, and let cool.

Drop the garlic into a food processor together with the drained eggplant pulp, fried peppers with their oil, parsley leaves, almonds, vinegar, extra virgin olive oil, and salt to taste. Pulse the motor on and off and, if needed, scrape the sides of the bowl with a spatula, until the mixture is smooth. If you like a more textured spread, process the peppers and all other ingredients in the blender, but use a food mill with the widest holes for the eggplants. Toss the eggplant and pepper mixture thoroughly in a bowl. Taste and add more salt or vinegar if needed.

Transfer the spread to a container, cover, and refrigerate overnight. The spread keeps for about 2 weeks in the refrigerator. Transfer to a serving plate, sprinkle with sumac if you like, and serve.

Feta and Pepper Spread

I always have this appetizer in my fridge, in either its green or red version, which I prepare in the summer with my small crop of sweet and hot green and red peppers. Serve with toasted whole wheat bread or with crudités.

Makes 8 to 10 servings as an appetizer

1/4 cup plus 2 tablespoons olive oil

1 large green bell pepper, coarsely chopped

1 or 2 small fresh green chiles, seeded and chopped

1 pound feta cheese, crumbled

1/4 cup Greek yogurt, preferably sheep's milk (see page 213)

1 large red bell pepper, coarsely chopped

1 to 2 teaspoons Aleppo or Maraş pepper, or a pinch of hot red pepper flakes, to taste

Warm half the olive oil in a skillet over medium-high heat, add the green pepper and chile, and sauté, stirring, for about 8 minutes, until soft. Transfer the sautéed peppers and their oil to a blender or food processor and add half the cheese and half the yogurt. Process until smooth. Transfer to one side of a serving dish.

Warm the rest of the oil in the skillet and sauté the red bell pepper and Aleppo pepper until soft. Process in the food processor with the rest of the cheese and yogurt and transfer to the other side of the serving bowl.

Cover and refrigerate. Keeps well for 2 to 3 weeks or more. Bring to room temperature before serving.

✦ Fried Mussels in Ouzo Batter ✦

Fried mussels were at the heart of the legendary meze spreads of Salonika, Greece's second-largest city, in the North. Many gourmands consider Salonika and the region of Macedonia the gastronomic center of Greece. Fresh mussels were scarce in Athens, before the extensive farming on the western shores of Macedonia. I must have been more than eighteen years old when I tasted a mussel for the first time, in a short visit to Salonika. I still remember the delicious plump golden-fried mollusks with the crunchy exterior and soft juicy core. They were served on a little plate, pinned with toothpicks and arranged in a circle around a dollop of garlic sauce. Much later, when I started cooking and receiving friends, I often passed around fried mussels on a large platter with a bowl of garlic sauce in the center. In her wonderful book *Mediterranean Street Food*, my friend Anissa Helou describes the fried mussel sandwiches of Istanbul, which are laced with tarator (garlic sauce) and garnished with lettuce leaves or tomato slices, much like burgers or gyro. After many tries and a few misses, I settled on this fragrant ouzo batter that was originally part of a recipe for bacalao fritters (salted cod).

Makes 4 to 6 servings as an appetizer

35 to 40 large mussels, cleaned under running water (about 3 pounds)

1 cup dry white wine (optional)

Sea salt

Good pinch of Aleppo or Maraş pepper or hot red pepper flakes, to taste

1 cup plus 2 tablespoons cornstarch

Olive oil or olive and sunflower oil for frying

$1^1/2$ cups all-purpose flour

$1^1/2$ teaspoons baking powder

1 cup ouzo (see Note)

$^1/2$ cup sparkling water, or more as needed

2 lemons, quartered

Vali's Skordalia (page 50) or Roasted Garlic Skordalia (page 51)

Place the mussels in a large pot over high heat and add the wine, if using. Cover and let the mussels steam for about 5 minutes, shaking the pot and stirring every now and then, until the shells open. Throw away the ones that stay closed. Shuck the mussels and discard the shells. Cover and refrigerate until needed, up to 3 hours.

Add salt and Aleppo pepper to the mussels, dust with about 2 tablespoons cornstarch, and toss to coat lightly.

Heat about 2 inches of olive oil in a skillet over medium-high heat.

Mix the remaining 1 cup cornstarch, the flour, and the baking powder in a bowl. Add the ouzo and sparkling water, whisking to incorporate. It should be runny. If too thick, add a little more sparkling water.

When the oil is very hot (about 350°F), dip a few mussels at a time in the batter, remove with tongs, and fry, turning them as they turn deep golden, about 1 minute total. Transfer to a plate lined with a double layer of paper towels to drain.

Serve with lemon quarters and skordalia.

Note
Ouzo, Pernod, and raki are strong anise-flavored alcoholic drinks. If not available, substitute vodka or grappa, adding a pinch of ground star or green anise to the batter.

✦ Falafel ✦

The popular chickpea fritters originated in Egypt, and Claudia Roden believes that they are a very old preparation, probably invented by Christian Copts, who ate them during their numerous fast days when any food derived from animals was prohibited. All the cultures who tasted falafel have incorporated it into their own cuisines, because it is so delicious and nourishing and is an ideal street food. In Israel falafel are the convenience food of choice, and Athenian supermarkets carry packaged falafel mix. In traditional Greek cooking we have our own version of *revithokeftedes* (chickpea patties), usually prepared with cooked mashed chickpeas. Needless to say, there are as many variations of falafel as there are cooks. In Egypt dried fava beans used to be the main ingredient, but they are not used today in Israel or in other Mediterranean countries because many inhabitants of the area carry a gene that makes them severely allergic to favas.

To serve falafel the Middle Eastern way, cut a pita in half, open the pocket, slide 3 or 4 falafel into each pita half, then add some chopped vegetables and a hot sauce like zhug (page 21) or tahini mixed with lemon juice and paprika. You can also serve the falafel on a plate, decorated with sprigs of parsley or cilantro. Present a couple of hot sauces on the side, together with bread and a salad.

Makes about 35 falafel, serving 6 to 8 as an appetizer

$2/3$ cup coarsely chopped onion

4 garlic cloves

2 or 3 jalapeño chiles, seeded and coarsely chopped

1 cup dried chickpeas, preferably peeled, soaked overnight

$1/3$ cup dried red lentils or yellow split peas, soaked for 3 hours

$1/4$ cup plus 2 tablespoons fine bulgur, soaked for 10 minutes and drained

1 teaspoon baking powder

2 or 3 scallions, including most of the green, coarsely chopped

$1/2$ cup coarsely chopped fresh cilantro

$1/3$ cup coarsely chopped fresh flat-leaf parsley

3 tablespoons cornstarch

1 to 2 teaspoons ground cumin seeds

$1 1/2$ teaspoons sea salt, or to taste

Freshly ground black pepper

Olive oil for deep-frying

Put the onion, garlic, chiles, chickpeas, lentils, and bulgur in a food processor and pulse to make a paste. Add the baking powder, scallions, cilantro, parsley, cornstarch, cumin, salt, and pepper to taste and pulse to chop and incorporate all ingredients. (You can make the falafel mixture coarse or fine, according to your taste. I prefer it somewhat coarse, but you can work it more, until completely smooth, if you like.) Wet your hands and shape tablespoons of the mixture into balls, then flatten them.

Heat 2 inches of olive oil in a deep skillet or small saucepan to 350°F and deep-fry a few falafel at a time, so that the temperature of the oil won't drop and make the patties soggy. Remove with a slotted spoon after the falafel turn golden brown, 2 to 3 minutes. Drain on paper towels. Serve hot.

Notes
The falafel mixture can be refrigerated for 2 to 3 days, but omit the cilantro and add it only when you are ready to cook, because it discolors quickly.

A special gadget for shaping falafel is available at Middle Eastern markets (see Sources).

Falafel, page 58

Sautéed Black Olives, page 62

✦ Sautéed Black Olives ✦

Greeks adore *throumbes,* the black olives that are cured with just coarse sea salt, lightly oiled, and sprinkled with savory, oregano, or rosemary (page 40). These olives are made with completely ripe fruits and have to be consumed within a week, because they don't keep well (extra salt preserves the ones you find in stores). Ancient Greeks also loved these olives: "Let them serve you with wrinkled, overripe olives," writes Archestratus, the first known food writer, who lived in Sicily in the fourth century B.C., when southern Italy was part of the Greater Greece.

In North Africa olives are dried in the sun to last through the winter. In Puglia, on the heel of the Italian boot, the local small ripe black olives are fried in olive oil without being cured, sprinkled with coarse salt, and served warm as an appetizer with plenty of crusty bread. In my recipe, juicy black olives are sautéed with onions, as is the custom in the Peloponnese, in southern mainland Greece. Serve as an appetizer or snack or pit and chop the olives to serve on toasted bread as bruschetta.

Makes 8 to 10 servings as an appetizer

1 pound throumbes (wrinkled black Greek olives, often called Thassos) or juicy black olives such as Kalamata or Italian Gaeta olives or a mixture of black and Niçoise olives

Olive oil for sautéing

1 large red or white onion, sliced

1 tablespoon fresh rosemary leaves or a mixture of dried oregano and thyme

1 to 2 teaspoons Aleppo or Maraş pepper, or hot red pepper flakes to taste

Briefly rinse the olives under cold running water, drain, and dry thoroughly on paper towels.

Heat about $1/2$ inch olive oil in a skillet over medium-high heat. Add the onion slices and sauté for 1 or 2 minutes to soften. Add the olives and sauté, stirring often, for about 5 minutes, or until soft and shiny. With a slotted spoon, transfer the olives and onion to a bowl, add the herbs, toss well, and serve warm or at room temperature.

The oil can be added to tomato sauces and stews. The olives will keep, covered, in the refrigerator for about 1 week. Let come to room temperature before serving.

Maltese Dried Bean Spread

At La Maltija—a lovely restaurant in Valletta, Malta's capital—I tasted this traditional Maltese specialty. I was asked if I wanted it spicy and was given a small bottle of Caribbean hot pepper sauce! Apparently modern cooks don't take the time to chop the tasty local fresh hot chiles for the dressing. Dried favas are traditionally cooked and mashed with their skins, but you can make it with peeled dried favas, canned favas, or white beans. A similar appetizer, called *bissara*, is served in Egypt. It is flavored with plenty of cumin and dried mint (see the variation).

Serve bigilla or bissara as an appetizer, with fresh vegetable crudités, crackers, or toasted crusty bread. Maltese bread, baked in wood-burning ovens, is wonderful.

Makes 4 to 6 servings as an appetizer

$1^1/2$ cups dried fava beans, soaked overnight and boiled in plenty of water until almost mushy, canned fava beans, or cooked white beans (see page 212)

$1^1/2$ to 3 teaspoons Aleppo or Maraş pepper, or a pinch of hot red pepper flakes, to taste

1 fresh jalapeño chile, minced

3 to 4 tablespoons red wine vinegar or sherry vinegar

$1/4$ cup plus 1 tablespoon fruity extra virgin olive oil

Sea salt and freshly ground black pepper

$1^1/2$ teaspoons minced garlic, or to taste

1 cup chopped fresh flat-leaf parsley, plus a few sprigs for garnish

Drain the cooked favas or beans and mash with a fork or put through the largest holes of a food mill.

To make the sauce, combine the Aleppo pepper, jalapeño, 3 tablespoons of the vinegar, the olive oil, and a pinch of salt in a bowl. Whisk to mix. Add the garlic and parsley, then the mashed favas or beans, and stir thoroughly. Taste and add more vinegar and/or salt and freshly ground black pepper to taste. Cover and refrigerate for at least 3 hours before serving, garnished with sprigs of parsley.

BISSARA (EGYPTIAN DRIED BEAN SPREAD)
Omit the parsley and add $1^1/2$ to 2 teaspoons ground cumin seeds and about 1 teaspoon dried mint or $1/2$ cup finely chopped fresh mint leaves. Garnish with sprigs of fresh mint.

✦ Hummus and Spicy Garlic Chickpeas ✦

In the colorful shops of the Carmel market in Tel Aviv, mountains of hummus are displayed between layers of whole cooked chickpeas, sprinkled with paprika and parsley. In restaurants, whole chickpeas are often served in the center of a plate of hummus. This gave me the idea to combine two different chickpea dishes: the extremely tasty *ceci all'aglio* (chickpeas with garlic), a traditional dish from Calabria—the southwestern tip of the Italian mainland—and *hummus bi tahini,* the ubiquitous dip or spread of Middle Eastern cuisine. Note that you need to prepare this a day before you plan to serve it if you start with dried chickpeas, but if you have frozen cooked chickpeas the spread can be whipped up in a few minutes. Serve accompanied with fresh or toasted pita bread and with tender raw vegetables. Makes 6 to 8 servings as an appetizer

$1/4$ cup olive oil, plus more fruity extra virgin olive oil to drizzle over the hummus if you like

5 garlic cloves, 2 minced

2 to 5 teaspoons Aleppo or Maraş pepper, or a pinch of hot red pepper flakes, to taste

$3^1/2$ cups cooked and drained chickpeas (see page 212)

Sea salt

$1^1/2$ to 2 teaspoons sweet Hungarian paprika

$1/2$ cup tahini (sesame paste)

3 tablespoons fresh lemon juice, or more to taste

$1/2$ to $1^1/2$ teaspoons freshly ground cumin

3 tablespoons chopped fresh cilantro or flat-leaf parsley (optional)

Warm the olive oil and the minced garlic with the Aleppo pepper in a deep skillet over medium-high heat until the garlic starts to color, about 1 minute. Add $1^1/2$ cups of the cooked chickpeas and some salt. Sauté, stirring often, until all liquid has evaporated. Taste, adjust the seasoning, and set aside or refrigerate, covered, for 3 to 5 days.

In a food processor or blender, process the rest of the chickpeas to obtain a smooth paste. Add the rest of the garlic, peeled, a little paprika, the tahini, lemon juice, salt, and cumin. Process to mix thoroughly and taste to adjust the seasoning.

You can store the hummus, covered, in the refrigerator for up to 5 days. When you are about to serve, transfer the hummus to a shallow bowl and make a well in the center. Add the chickpeas, sprinkle with paprika, drizzle with extra virgin olive oil, and, if you like, sprinkle with cilantro or parsley. Let come to room temperature before serving.

✦ Yogurt Cheese with Herbs ✦

Armenians, Lebanese, and other inhabitants of the Middle East like to prepare a simple fresh cheese by draining the liquid from yogurt. In the past, as there was no refrigeration, this cheese was heavily salted, formed into balls, and completely dried in the sun. Stored in clay jars, it would keep for months, even years. The hard, pebblelike balls were pounded in a mortar and sprinkled on salads and vegetable dishes.

The light and fragrant, mildly tangy yogurt cheese I make can be dried slightly in the refrigerator and preserved in olive oil. But it can also be enjoyed fresh with bread or crudités. Makes 8 to 10 servings as an appetizer

2 pounds (8 cups) Greek yogurt, preferably sheep's milk (see page 213)

1 garlic clove, minced

1 cup chopped fresh dill or a combination of dill, oregano, thyme, and/or parsley and rosemary leaves

1 to 2 teaspoons freshly ground white pepper

1 teaspoon sea salt, or to taste

To Preserve in Spicy Oil

2 or 3 dried peperoncini or other small chiles, slashed in half with scissors from tip to cup but left attached at the stem

1 or 2 Turkish bay leaves

Dried oregano or thyme sprigs

1 1/2 to 2 cups olive oil

Combine the yogurt, garlic, and dill in a bowl. Add pepper to taste and the salt and stir well to incorporate. Lay a double layer of cheesecloth or a kitchen towel in a bowl, pour the yogurt mixture into it, tie the ends together, and suspend over a bowl to drain in a cool place. I usually hang it with kitchen twine to a rack of my refrigerator, placing a bowl under it. Leave for about 12 hours.

Open the cheesecloth and carefully transfer the soft cheese to a platter or wooden board to serve.

To preserve yogurt cheese, press and roll 1 tablespoon of the soft cheese at a time between your palms to form little balls. Place them on a plate and refrigerate, uncovered, overnight, preferably for 24 hours, to dry out a little.

Pack the cheese balls in a jar, together with the chiles, bay leaves, and herb sprigs. Pour enough olive oil over the cheese to cover it. Seal and store in the refrigerator. The olive oil will partially solidify. Bring to room temperature before serving. Yogurt cheese will keep for about 2 months.

Sweet-and-Sour Eggplant, Celery, Tomato, and Caper Relish

I call it *relish* even though I could also call it *stew*. In my view, though, this intensely flavored Sicilian dish should be served in small quantities. It can be spread on toasted bread, with or without cheese, and it can be an accompaniment to grilled poultry or fish. The recipe I started from comes from Mary Taylor Simeti's superb book *Pomp and Sustenance: Twenty-Five Centuries of Sicilian Food*. As Mary explained to me, there is not one but several versions of caponata in Sicily, made with the best vegetables of the season. In the spring, for example, caponata is made with artichokes. Summer eggplant caponata is the king, of course, and in its older versions the sauce in which the eggplants macerate contains such exotic ingredients as cocoa powder. Make caponata at least a day in advance to let the flavors develop. Makes 6 to 8 servings as an appetizer

Sea salt

2 or 3 eggplants (about 2^{1}/2 pounds), cut into 2-inch cubes

1 cup olive oil, or more as needed

1 onion, sliced

2 bell peppers, preferably 1 red and 1 green, coarsely diced

2 to 3 teaspoons Aleppo or Maraş pepper, or a pinch of hot red pepper flakes, to taste

3 fresh leaf celery sprigs, chopped (see Note), or 3 small celery ribs, cut into ^{1}/2-inch pieces

^{1}/2 cup drained capers

1 cup green or brown small olives, such as Greek cracked olives (Nafplion), Gaeta, or picholine, pitted

3 to 4 tablespoons good-quality red wine vinegar

1 to 2 teaspoons honey or sugar, or more to taste

2 cups All-Purpose Greek Tomato Sauce (page 22)

One 4-inch piece fresh orange peel (optional)

^{1}/2 cup slivered almonds or pine nuts, toasted (see page 213)

Generously salt the eggplant cubes, toss, and drain in a colander for 1 hour, tossing once. Rinse under cold running water and pat dry with paper towels.

Preheat the broiler. Layer 2 baking sheets with parchment paper and place the eggplant cubes on the sheets in a single layer. (You may need to do this in 3 batches.) Drizzle each eggplant layer with olive oil and toss. Set the first baking sheet about 5 inches from the heat source. Broil, tossing twice, until golden and cooked through,

20 minutes or more. Continue with the rest of the eggplant. Alternatively, you can stir-fry the eggplant cubes in olive oil.

Warm $1/4$ cup olive oil in a large skillet or sauté pan over medium heat. Add the onion, sprinkle with salt, and sauté, stirring often, for 5 minutes or more, until translucent. Add the bell peppers, Aleppo pepper, and celery and continue to sauté, stirring often, for 10 to 15 minutes, until all the vegetables are wilted. Add the capers, the olives, 3 tablespoons of the vinegar, and 1 teaspoon of the honey and toss for 1 or 2 minutes. Pour in the tomato sauce, add the orange peel if you're using it, and bring to a boil. Lower the heat and simmer for 10 minutes. Add the eggplant and toss carefully to incorporate into the sauce. Bring slowly to a boil and boil for 5 minutes. Remove from the heat, taste, and add salt, vinegar, honey, and/or pepper.

Let cool completely and refrigerate overnight, preferably for 24 hours. Bring to room temperature, sprinkle with almonds, and serve.

Note
Leaf celery (*Apium graveolens* var. *secalinum*) is also called *Chinese celery, wild celery,* and *French celery.* It looks like oversized thick parsley and has an intense aroma and flavor. You can occasionally find it at Chinese markets and specialty stores.

❖ Skillet Shrimp Two Ways ❖

A Moroccan and a Spanish way to serve shrimp, both equally delicious, easy, and fast. You can also serve these shrimp as a main course, accompanied by steamed potatoes. I prefer not to peel small or medium shrimp, because I think they are more flavorful cooked in their shell. But you can peel them if you like.

Whichever sauce the shrimp are cooked in, if you present them as an appetizer, serve them in the middle of the table with plenty of fresh crusty bread to dip into the scrumptious juices.

With Chermoula

Of the many variations of *chermoula*, a classic Moroccan herb and spice marinade, this is my favorite. Chermoula is used primarily for fish and seafood (skewered chunks of tuna, salmon, or other fish, whole or filleted, as well as shrimp; see page 105), but it works well with poultry, especially with chicken breast or thigh fillets. It can also be used as a dressing for grilled or fried eggplant, zucchini, and other vegetables.

Makes 6 to 8 servings as an appetizer, 4 as a main course

CHERMOULA

3 garlic cloves, peeled

3 to 5 tablespoons Harissa (page 19) or chile paste

$1/2$ cup coarsely chopped fresh cilantro

$1/2$ cup coarsely chopped fresh flat-leaf parsley

1 teaspoon ground cumin

2 tablespoons sweet Hungarian paprika

2 tablespoons red wine vinegar

3 tablespoons balsamic vinegar

$1/4$ cup olive oil

SHRIMP

$1^1/2$ pounds medium shrimp, peeled if you like, but tails left on, and deveined

3 tablespoons olive oil

Lemon wedges for serving

Place the garlic, harissa, cilantro, parsley, cumin, paprika, vinegars, and $1/4$ cup of the olive oil in a food processor and process to make a paste. Toss the shrimp with the paste in a bowl, cover, and refrigerate for 30 to 60 minutes.

Heat the remaining 3 tablespoons olive oil in a large skillet over medium-high heat and add the shrimp. Cook, tossing often, until firm and pink, about 5 minutes. Serve immediately with lemon wedges.

(continued)

Gambas al Ajillo (Shrimp with Garlic, Chile, Sherry, and Parsley)

This irresistible Catalan tapas dish is brought to the table sizzling in a *cazuela,* the ceramic pan in which the shrimp are traditionally cooked. You can imitate the effect by heating an ovenproof clay pan in the oven and transferring the cooked shrimp to it for serving. Place the extra-hot pan on a large wooden platter or on a tray lined with a thick pad. If it is an appetizer, serve in the middle of the table with plenty of crusty bread. The sauce is sublime.

Makes 6 to 8 servings as an appetizer, 4 as a main course

$1/3$ cup olive oil

5 garlic cloves, thinly sliced, or more to taste

2 dried guindillas or chiles de árbol, halved lengthwise, 2 to 4 teaspoons Aleppo or Maraş pepper, or a pinch of hot red pepper flakes, to taste

$1^1/2$ pounds medium shrimp, peeled if you like, but tails left on, and deveined

$1/2$ cup dry sherry or a combination of brandy and dry white wine

3 to 4 tablespoons fresh lemon juice, to taste

$1/2$ cup chopped fresh flat-leaf parsley

Good pinch of Spanish smoked paprika (pimentón; optional)

Good pinch of salt, preferably fleur de sel

Lemon wedges for serving

Heat the olive oil in a skillet over medium-high heat. Add the garlic and guindillas and cook briefly, until the garlic is just starting to color. Add the shrimp and cook, tossing with a spatula, for 3 to 5 minutes, until the shrimp are firm and pink. Add the sherry, 3 tablespoons of the lemon juice, and the parsley. Toss and, as the liquid starts to bubble, remove the pan from the heat. Sprinkle the shrimp with the smoked paprika if you like and with salt and take to the table immediately in the skillet or in a heated clay dish. Add more lemon juice if you like and pass the lemon wedges around.

Tunisian Meat or Cheese Pies

I have deliberately avoided the use of commercial frozen phyllo in this book's recipes because the phyllo available in the United States is quite unpredictable, to say the least. Even here, in my Greek kitchen, although I have a choice of several kinds of phyllo sheets, frozen or fresh, in various thicknesses, I feel store-bought phyllo is tasteless and inferior to homemade. I know that very few people have the ability to roll paper-thin sheets, but I much prefer the crudest hand-rolled phyllo to the flavorless commercial variety. I don't intend to drag you into the intricate art of phyllo rolling, however.

Fortunately this traditional North African pastry is so easy to make that you will love it even if you have never before tried to make a pastry crust. The detailed instructions come from Anissa Helou's *Savory Baking from the Mediterranean.* I have altered Anissa's meat filling a bit, lightening it with some grated carrot, and I added pine nuts, following the fried Lebanese samboosak as described in Helou's unsurpassed first book, *Lebanese Cuisine.* The simple cheese filling is inspired by Moroccan fried phyllo triangles. Note that a very similar pastry can be used for cookies filled with dates or other dried fruit, according to Salima Hadjiat's book *La Cuisine d'Algerie.*

Serve meat or cheese samboosak with drinks. It is an ideal finger food, and you can complement it with Sweet-and-Sour Eggplants with Nuts, Sultanas, Basil, and Peperoncino (page 49) or Ezme Salatasi (page 84). I also like to serve the little pies with Tunisian Carrot Salad or North African Zucchini or Squash Salad (page 87) on a meze spread. Makes about 45 small pies

3^1/2 cups fine semolina flour

1^1/2 teaspoons sea salt

^{1}/3 cup olive oil

1 cup warm water

1 recipe Meat or Cheese Filling for Samboosak (recipes follow)

In the bowl of a stand mixer, combine the semolina and salt. Add the olive oil and pulse briefly with the dough hook to incorporate. With the motor running, add the warm water and work for 1 or 2 minutes, until a rough dough forms. Cover with plastic wrap and let rest for 15 minutes. Work the dough again for 1 to 2 minutes, until smooth and elastic, then cover and let rest for 1 hour.

Meanwhile, make the filling.

Turn the dough onto a very lightly floured work surface and knead for 1 minute. Divide in two, cover the pieces with plastic wrap, and let rest for 10 to 15 minutes. Roll one of the pieces with a rolling pin to about $1/4$-inch thickness. With a 3-inch pastry cutter, cut as many disks as possible from the pastry. Gather the leftover dough, roll again, and cut more disks.

Preheat the oven to 400°F and line 2 baking sheets with parchment paper.

Place 1 teaspoon of filling in the center of each disk, wet the edges with water, and fold to cover the filling and create half-moon pies. Press the border with the tines of a fork to seal and decorate the samboosak. Transfer to the lined baking sheets. Continue with the rest of the dough and filling—you may need more than 2 baking sheets.

Bake both sheets together for 15 minutes, then switch the position of the sheets and bake for another 10 to 15 minutes, until golden. Serve hot, warm, or at room temperature. The pies keep for a week in a sealed container in the refrigerator and can also be frozen.

Meat Filling for Samboosak

3 tablespoons olive oil

$2/3$ cup grated carrot

7 ounces ground beef

1 teaspoon Baharat (page 12) or ground allspice, or more to taste

$1/2$ to 1 teaspoon freshly ground black pepper

Sea salt

$1/4$ cup toasted pine nuts (see page 213)

2 teaspoons fresh lemon juice or pomegranate molasses

Warm the olive oil in a medium skillet over medium-high heat. Add the carrot and sauté, tossing often, for 3 to 5 minutes, until wilted. Add the meat and sauté, tossing often and breaking up the lumps, until the meat is cooked through, about 10 minutes. Add the baharat, pepper, and salt to taste, and cook for a few more minutes, until the mixture dries. Add the pine nuts and lemon juice and taste to correct the seasoning. Let cool before filling the pies.

The filling can be prepared 2 to 5 days in advance and kept covered in the refrigerator. Bring to room temperature before using.

Cheese Filling for Samboosak

7 ounces fresh goat cheese or feta, crumbled

$^1/2$ cup juicy black olives, pitted, rinsed to rid them of extra salt, drained on paper towels, and chopped

$^2/3$ cup chopped fresh cilantro

Pinch of Aleppo or Maraş pepper or hot red pepper flakes, to taste

2 medium eggs

In a bowl, combine the cheese, olives, cilantro, and Aleppo pepper. Add the eggs and stir well to incorporate.

Sweet and Savory Meatballs

I first came across this old unusual recipe many years ago, in the marvelous book *Bitter Almonds: Recollections and Recipes from a Sicilian Girlhood,* where Mary Taylor Simeti recorded Maria Grammatico's life story. Recently I found a similar recipe in Alba Pezone's column in the French *Elle à Table* magazine. Pezone has an Italian cooking school in Paris and called the meatballs *bonbons de viande* (meat bonbons). According to her, the recipe was traditionally prepared on Easter, by her Neapolitan grandmother.

Sweet-and-savory dishes were very common in ancient times and up until the Middle Ages and the Renaissance. We have descriptions of recipes where pieces of meat, together with spices, dried grapes or other fruits, and nuts, were pounded in big mortars in the kitchens of medieval castles. A mortar and pestle was, in fact, the most important kitchen tool in those days. As I chop the ingredients for the meatballs in my blender, I can't help thinking about the poor kitchen helpers who sweated for hours on end pounding ingredients for this and other dainty dishes served to the gentry.

My recipe is inspired by Grammatico's and Pezone's. I don't fry but rather broil the meatballs. Nor do I use tomato sauce as the Sicilian version suggests. I think you will love these meat *bonbons,* which can be prepared in advance, refrigerated or even frozen, and reheated just before serving. Make them quite small, if you have the time, and for a very attractive presentation, follow Pezone's suggestion: top each meatball with a leaf of parsley and prick with a toothpick. Makes 8 to 10 servings as an appetizer

1 cup sultanas (golden raisins)

1 cup white wine, preferably sweet, such as Greek Samos

1 cup almonds

2 large garlic cloves, peeled

3 cups stale whole wheat bread crumbs

2 pounds ground lamb or a combination of lean beef and pork with some fat

2 cups grated pecorino Romano cheese

$1/2$ cup pine nuts

$2/3$ cup finely chopped fresh flat-leaf parsley, plus leaves for garnish

Grated zest of 2 lemons, preferably organic

1 cup whole-milk yogurt

3 eggs, lightly beaten

1 teaspoon salt, or more to taste

1 teaspoon freshly ground black pepper, or
    more to taste

Olive oil for brushing the meatballs

Lemon wedges for serving

Place the sultanas in a bowl and pour the wine over them. Toss and set aside for 15 minutes or so to soften.

Put the almonds, garlic, and bread crumbs in a food processor or blender and chop, turning the motor on and off to make a coarse mixture. Drain the sultanas, pressing with your hands to extract the liquid. Add to the food processor and pulse very briefly just to chop the sultanas coarsely with the almond mixture, not to make a paste.

In a large bowl, toss the ground meat with the cheese and the mixture from the food processor. Stir in the pine nuts, parsley, lemon zest, yogurt, eggs, salt, and pepper.

Knead with your hands to mix thoroughly. Cover with plastic wrap and refrigerate for 1 hour or overnight.

Preheat the oven to 400°F. Line 2 baking sheets with parchment paper.

Roll heaping tablespoons of the meat mixture with your hands into balls. Make them smaller or larger, according to how much time you want to spend forming them. Place one next to the other on the lined baking sheets and brush liberally with olive oil, turning them to oil all sides.

Place both baking sheets in the oven and bake for 20 minutes. Switch the position of the baking sheets and bake for about 10 minutes more, or until the meatballs are deep golden and firm.

Let cool a little and transfer to a serving platter. Squeeze some lemon over them and serve. If you are presenting them on a buffet, place a leaf of parsley on each meatball and prick with a toothpick.

✦ Spicy Bulgur Salad ✦
with Nuts and Tomato Paste Dressing

This hearty salad became our standard picnic dish. We always make it the night before for our lunch on the beach with friends. Grilled fish or lamb chops on our small portable BBQ is the main dish, but everybody raves about the bulgur salad. Kostis, our friend and partner at Kea Artisanal, is eager to take the leftovers because he loves it even more than we do. The recipe is based on *Bazargan,* a Syrian-Jewish salad that Claudia Roden included in *A Book of Middle Eastern Food.* I first tasted it many years ago, during a food conference, and I was immediately fascinated by this earthy, fragrant, and crunchy sweet-and-sour mixture. Claudia whipped it up during a cooking demo, and as she gave us tastings she pointed out that the salad was not ready because it had to sit for a few hours so that the grains could soak up the flavors from the sauce and the spices. Reading the recipe in Claudia's old book, I wasn't tempted to try it—one of my very few such misses. I am so glad I had the chance to taste it, so now I am passing the torch.

Makes 8 to 10 servings as an appetizer

$2^2/3$ cups coarse bulgur, soaked in cold water for 20 to 30 minutes, or until tender

$3/4$ cup extra virgin olive oil

3 tablespoons pomegranate molasses, or juice of 1 lemon, or more to taste

$1/4$ cup plus 2 tablespoons tomato paste

2 teaspoons ground cumin

2 tablespoons ground coriander seeds

$1/2$ to 1 teaspoon ground allspice

$1/2$ to 1 teaspoon cayenne, or 1 to 3 teaspoons Aleppo or Maraş pepper, or a pinch of hot red pepper flakes, to taste

Sea salt

1 cup coarsely ground walnuts

1 cup coarsely ground toasted hazelnuts (see page 213)

$1/2$ cup coarsely ground toasted salted almonds (see page 213)

$1/2$ cup toasted pine nuts (see page 213)

$2/3$ cup chopped fresh cilantro or flat-leaf parsley

8 to 10 medium romaine lettuce leaves (optional)

TOPPINGS (OPTIONAL)

1 small sweet onion, chopped

$1/3$ cup sliced or chopped fresh or pickled red or green chiles

Drain the bulgur well in a strainer lined with cheesecloth and pat with paper towels to extract all the water.

In a bowl, whisk together the olive oil, pomegranate molasses, tomato paste, and spices, adding salt sparingly.

In a large bowl, mix the bulgur with the nuts and add the cilantro. Pour the oil mixture over the bulgur mixture and toss well. Cover and refrigerate for at least 3 hours, preferably overnight. Taste and adjust the seasoning just before serving, preferably at room temperature. If you are using the toppings, toss half with the bulgur at the last minute. Spoon onto lettuce leaves if you like or serve in a bowl, sprinkling with the rest of the toppings. The bulgur salad keeps well in the refrigerator for about 4 days.

VARIATIONS

Instead of soaking the bulgur in water, you can place the grain in a bowl and pour 1 quart warm tomato juice over it. Let sit for 15 to 20 minutes to absorb the juice, toss well, and continue adding the rest of the ingredients as directed.

Add $1^1/2$ cups Dukkah (page 15), omitting the cumin and coriander and reducing the hazelnuts to $1/2$ cup.

Spicy Bulgur Salad with Nuts and Tomato Paste Dressing, page 78

Mixed Salad with Orange, Lemon, Chile, and Honey Vinaigrette, page 82

Mixed Salad with Orange, Lemon, Chile, and Honey Vinaigrette

The combination of orange, chiles, lemon, honey, and mustard make a wonderfully versatile dressing. You can use any combination of fresh and/or steamed vegetables, such as broccoli, cauliflower, and endive, butter lettuce, radishes, or tender spinach leaves in the salad. Makes 6 to 8 servings as an appetizer

DRESSING

2 tablespoons fresh orange juice

2 tablespoons fresh lemon juice

1 teaspoon ground yellow mustard seeds, or $1/2$ teaspoon dry mustard

1 tablespoon Lemon, Honey, and Pepper Jelly (page 26), or 1 more teaspoon lemon juice and 1 teaspoon honey

$1/4$ cup plus 1 tablespoon fruity extra virgin olive oil

2 to 3 tablespoons chopped fresh or pickled chile or Peperoncini sott'Olio (page 36), to taste

Sea salt and freshly ground black pepper to taste

2 tablespoons grated orange or lemon zest

SALAD

Tender and crisp leaves from the heart of a head of romaine lettuce, coarsely chopped

1 small fennel bulb, outer leaves and tops discarded, thinly sliced lengthwise

1 bunch of arugula, coarsely chopped

1 small orange, peeled and sliced

6 to 8 small unsprayed nasturtium leaves and a few flowers (optional)

2 or 3 kumquats, thinly sliced and seeded (optional)

1 large or 2 small beets (about $1/2$ pound), boiled or baked, peeled, and sliced

2 to 3 tablespoons toasted pine nuts (see page 213)

To make the dressing, mix the orange and lemon juices with the mustard, jelly, and olive oil; beat to combine. Add the chile, salt, pepper, and zest. Taste and adjust the seasoning.

In a large bowl, toss together the lettuce, fennel, arugula, and orange slices, adding the nasturtium leaves and kumquats if you're using them. Reserve 1 tablespoon of the dressing and pour the rest over the greens and toss well. Add the beet slices carefully, because they stain all surrounding ingredients, and drizzle them with the reserved dressing. Sprinkle with the pine nuts, decorate with the nasturtium flowers if you're using them, and serve immediately.

Israeli Macerated Salad

This unusual salad of cabbage and other vegetables is refrigerated overnight to wilt with coarse salt and lemon juice infused with chopped jalapeños, which give it a spicy zing. It is served at Doctor Chakchouka, a small, informal restaurant in Jaffa, the picturesque historic district of Tel Aviv. Bino Gabso, the restaurant's owner, serves Libyan Jewish food based on his mother's recipes. Add as many chiles as you like, according to how hot you want the salad. Olive oil is not necessary; this salad is just as tasty without it. Makes 8 to 10 servings as an appetizer

1 small tender green cabbage (about 2 pounds), coarsely shredded

1 large green bell pepper, julienned

2 cups tender cauliflower florets and/or Pink Cauliflower and Turnip Pickles (page 39)

3 medium carrots, thinly sliced, or 8 to 10 tender baby carrots

1 daikon, thinly sliced (optional)

1 very small tender fennel bulb, thinly sliced

3 or 4 jalapeño chiles, seeded and chopped

6 to 8 pickled small green chiles

1 1/2 teaspoons coarse sea salt

3 tablespoons fresh lemon juice, or more to taste

3 tablespoons extra virgin olive oil (optional)

Place the cabbage, bell pepper, cauliflower if you're using fresh, carrots, daikon, fennel, and chiles in a large bowl. Sprinkle with the salt and toss thoroughly with your hands for 1 minute. (Wear rubber gloves if chiles irritate your skin.) Add the lemon juice, toss a few more times, cover with plastic wrap, and refrigerate for 4 to 5 hours or overnight, up to 4 days.

Just before serving, toss once more, discard most of the accumulated juices, and taste. Adjust the seasoning by adding a little more lemon juice and some olive oil if you like. If you're using pickled cauliflower florets and turnips, add them only at the last minute, because they stain the surrounding salad.

Spicy Tomato, Pepper, Cucumber, Mint, and Parsley Salad

This is the standard salad-relish you find in every tavern and restaurant in Istanbul. It accompanies grilled meat and especially kebabs. Turkish food is often eaten with a spoon, and so is this salad—all its ingredients are finely chopped. Instead of a simple lemon vinaigrette, which is the most common dressing, I like to add a little balsamic vinegar and lemon zest. Add as much jalapeño as you like, but bear in mind that this Turkish salsa is meant to be refreshing and not overpoweringly hot.

Makes 4 to 6 servings as an appetizer

Uses: Serve as a side dish with grilled meat, poultry, or fish. You can also spread it on toasted country bread to make light and delicious crostini.

SALAD

3 medium ripe fresh red tomatoes

1/2 English cucumber, quartered lengthwise and finely sliced

1/2 cup tightly packed coarsely chopped purslane or arugula

2 scallions, including most of the green, thinly sliced

1 cup tightly packed coarsely chopped fresh flat-leaf parsley

3 tablespoons chopped fresh mint leaves

1 to 2 tablespoons chopped fresh thyme or savory

2 to 4 jalapeño chiles, seeded and finely diced

2 tablespoons capers, preferably salt-packed, rinsed well and drained (optional)

DRESSING

3 tablespoons fruity extra virgin olive oil

1 tablespoon fresh lemon juice

1 tablespoon balsamic vinegar

2 teaspoons grated lemon zest

Sea salt and freshly ground black pepper

Pinch of sumac (optional)

Cut the tomatoes in half crosswise and squeeze lightly to remove the seeds. With a serrated knife, dice the tomatoes and transfer to a strainer to drain.

In a salad bowl, mix together the cucumber, greens, scallions, herbs, jalapeños, and capers. Add the tomatoes.

To make the dressing, whisk together the olive oil, lemon juice, vinegar, lemon zest, and salt and pepper to taste. Pour over the salad and toss. Taste and adjust the seasoning. Refrigerate for 20 to 30 minutes to give the flavors time to meld. Sprinkle with sumac before serving if you like.

VARIATION

By adding crumbled toasted pita or pieces of toasted whole wheat bread, and maybe some crumbled feta, you can turn ezme into mechouia, a common Middle Eastern bread salad.

✦ Tunisian Carrot Salad ✦

The mashed vegetable salads of North Africa have a complex, deep flavor that belies how easy they are to make. Spicy harissa, fresh cilantro, lemon juice, and caraway seeds add extra dimensions to the vegetable puree that is traditionally served as an appetizer but is also an ideal accompaniment to grilled meat, poultry, or fish. Tunisian Carrot Salad is by far the best of these salads, but squash and zucchini salads are equally wonderful (see the variations). Makes 4 servings as an appetizer

1 pound carrots

2 garlic cloves, minced, or 1 teaspoon roasted garlic paste (page 51)

2 to 3 tablespoons fresh lemon juice

$1/2$ to 1 teaspoon Harissa (page 19) or any hot pepper paste

$1^1/2$ teaspoons ground caraway seeds, preferably freshly ground

$1/2$ cup chopped fresh cilantro leaves

3 to 4 tablespoons olive oil

Sea salt

A few Kalamata olives for garnish

$1/2$ cup diced feta cheese (optional)

1 or 2 Lemon Slices in Spicy Olive Oil (optional; page 33)

Peel the carrots, chop coarsely, and transfer to a saucepan. Cover the carrots with cold water and bring to a boil. Reduce the heat to low, and simmer the carrots until tender, about 20 minutes. Drain, then mash with a fork or pass through a food mill fitted with the medium disk into a large bowl. Mix in the garlic, 2 tablespoons of the lemon juice, the harissa, the caraway, and the cilantro. Stir in the olive oil and salt to taste. Taste and add lemon, salt, or harissa as needed. Let cool and refrigerate for at least 3 hours or overnight.

Just before serving, decorate with olives and feta and chopped lemon slices if you like.

NORTH AFRICAN ZUCCHINI OR SQUASH SALAD

Steam or boil 2 pounds medium zucchini or squash in salted water until tender. Mash with a fork, place the pulp in a fine strainer, and let it drain for 20 to 30 minutes, until most of the liquid has run off. Mix with the rest of the ingredients as directed, substituting 3 tablespoons chopped fresh mint leaves for the cilantro.

Yogurt, Spinach, and Parsley Salad with Walnuts

As is the case with some Mediterranean dishes, the term *borani* means different things in the countries of the region. Spinach, eggplant, zucchini, or any other vegetable mixed with yogurt is the most common borani, both in the Middle East and in the Balkans. The dish originates in Persia (Iran), and its name is believed to derive from a Persian queen who was fond of yogurt. But in the Gaziantep, in Turkish Anatolia, borani is a dish that combines black-eyed peas, ground meat, and chard (see page 157). The recipe that follows mixes both cooked spinach and fresh parsley and cilantro and is my adaptation of an Armenian dish. In Israel you will often find a vivid pink borani made with beets and beet greens instead of spinach (see the variation). As an alternative to the traditional pita bread, I prefer to spread borani on toasted whole wheat or multigrain bread rubbed with a cut clove of garlic. Borani can also be a side dish, accompanying poached or grilled fish or chicken. Makes about 3 cups

1 1/2 pounds spinach leaves, coarsely chopped

1 cup chopped fresh flat-leaf parsley

1/2 cup chopped fresh cilantro

3 cups Greek yogurt, preferably sheep's milk (see page 213)

2 or 3 garlic cloves, minced, to taste

1 to 3 jalapeño chiles, finely chopped, to taste

Sea salt and freshly ground black pepper

1/2 cup coarsely chopped walnuts

Wash the spinach in a saucepan and place it over high heat. Cover and steam it until wilted in the water that clings to the leaves, 2 to 3 minutes. Toss once or twice while cooking and be careful not to let it burn. Remove the spinach from the heat, turn it into a colander, and let it cool and drain. Press with your hands to remove as much liquid as possible. Finely chop the spinach and transfer to a bowl.

Add the parsley, cilantro, yogurt, garlic, and chiles, stirring well. Add a little salt, taste, and add more if necessary along with a little black pepper. Cover and refrigerate for at least 3 hours or overnight.

Spread on toasts, sprinkle with walnuts, and serve as an appetizer or transfer to a serving dish and sprinkle with walnuts.

PINK BORANI WITH BEETS

Dice 4 or 5 cooked and peeled large beets (together with their cooked stems and greens, if you like) and mix with the garlic, yogurt, and jalapeños (as directed). Omit the parsley and cilantro and flavor with $1/2$ cup chopped fresh dill and the grated zest of $1/2$ lemon. I add 2 to 3 tablespoons fresh lemon juice, as beets are a little sweet for my taste, but you may not agree.

Yogurt, Spinach, and Parsley
Salad with Walnuts, page 88

Grilled Pepper Salad with Feta and Cilantro, page 92

Grilled Bell Peppers in Anchovy and Peperoncino Olive Oil

Although bell peppers are New World vegetables and became part of the Mediterranean food basket quite late—sometime in the mid-eighteenth century—it is hard to imagine how we did without them. Today they are added to sauces, fried, and stuffed with rice, vegetables, meat, or fish. They are also grilled and eaten simply with bread and cheese or as an accompaniment to meat, poultry, or fish. Here is the simplest way to grill and peel bell peppers, and two variations on the basic recipe: grilled pepper salad with feta and cilantro and grilled pepper rolls with tyrokafteri (feta cheese spread). All three make colorful and delicious appetizers. Makes 8 to 10 servings as an appetizer

3 red bell peppers

3 green bell peppers

3 yellow bell peppers

1/4 cup extra virgin olive oil

1 tablespoon Anchovy and Peperoncino Olive Oil (page 31), or 2 or 3 anchovy fillets mashed with 1 tablespoon olive oil

2 to 3 tablespoons sherry vinegar, to taste

1/2 teaspoon freshly ground black pepper

Cut the peppers lengthwise into thirds, seed them, and discard the stems. Each pepper should yield 3 quite flat pieces.

Position an oven rack about 5 inches from the broiler, line the rack with aluminum foil, and lay the pepper pieces, skin side up, on the foil. Broil the peppers for 15 to 20 minutes, until their skins are black and blistered. Place the peppers in a bowl and cover with plastic wrap. Leave for about 5 minutes, then peel off the blackened skin.

In a bowl, whisk the olive oil with the Anchovy and Peperoncino Olive Oil and 2 tablespoons of the vinegar. Place alternating layers of red, green, and yellow pepper pieces on a platter and drizzle with the sauce. Sprinkle with ground pepper and taste, adding more vinegar if desired.

The peppers will keep, covered, for about 2 weeks in the refrigerator. The oil will solidify. Bring to room temperature before serving.

Grilled Pepper Salad with Feta and Cilantro

Makes 4 to 6 servings

9 pieces Grilled Bell Peppers (preceding recipe), preferably red

1 tablespoon balsamic vinegar

3 tablespoons extra virgin olive oil

1 cup coarsely crumbled feta cheese

1/2 cup chopped fresh cilantro

Lettuce leaves for serving (optional)

Good pinch of Aleppo or Maraş pepper or hot red pepper flakes or freshly ground black pepper, to taste

Cut each pepper piece lengthwise into strips. Toss with the vinegar and olive oil, add the feta and cilantro, and toss again. Place the lettuce leaves in a bowl if you're using them and add the pepper strip mixture. Sprinkle with Aleppo pepper and serve.

Grilled Pepper Rolls with Tyrokafteri

Makes 30 rolls

15 pieces Grilled Bell Peppers (preceding recipe) of various colors

1 cup Pepper and Feta Spread (page 55)

2 tablespoons toasted almonds (see page 213), coarsely ground (optional)

Fresh flat-leaf parsley sprigs for garnish (optional)

Drain the grilled pepper pieces thoroughly and cut each in half lengthwise. Place a bit less than a teaspoon of the feta spread at the end of a pepper strip and roll it up crosswise, like a cigar. Secure with a toothpick. Refrigerate for 1 or 2 hours or overnight. Sprinkle with almonds and garnish with parsley sprigs if you like, and serve.

Paximadi Salad with Tomatoes, Feta, and Capers

The Arab *fattoush,* made with toasted pita, and *panzanella* and its numerous versions in the Italian North and South are two of the most familiar Mediterranean bread salads. But I chose to give you this Greek salad, because I—together with all our foreign visitors who have tasted it over the years—find it irresistible. *Paximadi* (plural *paximadia*) is the barley rusk, the Greek twice-baked hard biscuit, which was for centuries a staple for islanders and sailors in the parts of Greece where wheat is difficult to grow and wood for firing the oven was scarce. Paximadia can be baked every three months or even once or twice a year, as they keep practically indefinitely. Almost forgotten when the country became affluent—from the 1970s, as white bread conquered all homes—paximadia are now the "in" food item. Rusks baked entirely with barley flour—also called *Cretan paximadia* because they were always obtainable in Crete—need to be soaked briefly in water to soften; otherwise you may break your teeth trying to bite into them. Now most Athenian bakeries sell countless versions of lighter, crunchy paximadia, baked with combinations of wheat, barley, and other flours.

For this salad the original hard barley rusks are needed—and fortunately they are imported to the United States (see Sources). The crumbled hard rusks acquire a superb flavor and texture from steeping in the juices of the chopped tomatoes and the spicy aromatic olive oil sauce. Lighter biscuits get mushy. Prepare the salad one to three hours in advance, but toss it just before serving. Paximadi salad makes a delicious summer lunch on its own, perfect for picnics at the beach. I make it in a large container and serve it under the beach umbrella in our attractive reusable plastic picnic bowls. The chunky salad can be eaten with a spoon or fork, and we often enjoy it sipping the crisp fruity white or rosé wine that we take to the beach in a cooler.

Makes 6 to 8 servings as an appetizer

(continued)

4 cups paximadia in bite-sized pieces (see Notes)

2 pounds ripe but firm summer tomatoes (see Notes)

1 white onion, thinly sliced (about 2 cups)

1 cup fresh purslane leaves (optional)

3 tablespoons drained capers

$^1/_2$ cup fresh basil leaves, torn or coarsely chopped, tender flat-leaf parsley leaves, or a combination of parsley and fresh oregano or thyme

$2^1/_2$ cups diced feta cheese (about 10 ounces)

1 tablespoon dried Greek oregano

DRESSING

2 tablespoons balsamic vinegar, or to taste

$^1/_2$ cup extra virgin olive oil

3 or 4 pickled peperoncini or other chiles, minced

Zest of 1 lemon, preferably organic (optional)

Freshly ground black pepper

Sea salt (optional)

Spread the paximadia in the bottom of a salad bowl or other container. Using a sharp serrated knife, cut the tomatoes into roughly $1^1/_2$-inch pieces over the paximadia so the bread collects the juices. Arrange the onion rings and purslane, if you're using it, over the tomatoes, then sprinkle on the capers and basil. Top with the feta and sprinkle with the oregano.

To make the dressing, whisk the vinegar and olive oil together in a bowl and add the chiles, lemon zest if you're using it, a few grindings of pepper and salt if you like (the capers and feta are quite salty, so you may not need extra).

Cover the dressing and let stand for 1 hour in a cool place. I don't like to refrigerate a salad with tomatoes, but you will probably need to if you won't be eating it within the hour and the weather is hot. Toss the salad with the dressing thoroughly at the last minute and serve in bowls.

Notes

You can substitute stale whole wheat sourdough or any other heavy, chewy bread for the paximadia. Cut into thick slices, dice, and toast in the oven to dry.

To break hard paximadia into pieces, wrap in a clean tea towel and beat with a pestle or rolling pin. Add the pieces and crumbs to the salad.

This salad calls for full-flavored tomatoes, which means they should not have been refrigerated. Use big tomatoes or small, any color, or a combination of different heirloom tomatoes.

Cold Almond and Garlic Soup

Although the ajo blanco served today is very mild, I'm sure that in its medieval form it was much spicier. I make this cold soup from Spain frequently during the summer because I find its taste irresistible, especially with the extra bite given by the fresh ginger. The quality of the almonds plays a very important role, so I suggest you don't use peeled supermarket almonds but the very flavorful Spanish Marcona almonds that you can get in specialty stores. Peeling them is very easy, but if you have to use blanched almonds, let them soak in cold water for a couple of hours or overnight. Instead of the water the original recipe required, I use homemade chicken stock.

Makes 4 servings

1 cup almonds, peeled (see Note)

1 or 2 garlic cloves, peeled and halved lengthwise

$1/2$ to 1 teaspoon sea salt

$1^1/2$ cups toasted whole wheat or multigrain bread crumbs

3 cups defatted homemade chicken stock

1 to 2 tablespoons grated fresh ginger, to taste

$1/4$ cup plus 1 tablespoon extra virgin olive oil

2 tablespoons sherry vinegar

Freshly ground white pepper

4 to 8 fresh flat-leaf parsley or cilantro sprigs

Red and green grapes for garnish

Place the almonds and garlic in a food processor or blender. Add the salt and process to a smooth paste. If necessary, add a few tablespoons of water. Add the bread crumbs and a little chicken stock to the mixture. Process again for a few seconds.

Add the grated ginger, olive oil, and vinegar to the almond mixture. Process again, adding the remaining stock to make a creamy soup. Add white pepper to taste.

Transfer the soup to a covered container and refrigerate for 2 to 3 hours or overnight. Stir well before serving and garnish each bowl with sprigs of parsley or cilantro and some fresh red and green grapes.

Note
To peel the almonds, blanch them for 1 or 2 minutes in boiling water, drain, and rub with your fingers to remove the skins.

Cold Tomato, Garlic, and Bread Soup

I am tediously frugal when it comes to the vegetables I grow in my garden. I try to use every last bit of my precious tomatoes, even the ones that are half eaten by wasps and grasshoppers—usually the most gorgeous of my crop. With those and some leftover bits from our everyday salad, I whip up my take on *salmorejo*, the thick cold tomato soup from Córdoba, in Andalusia. Similar to gazpacho but thicker, salmorejo is traditionally topped with slices of Iberian ham and/or hard-boiled eggs. I often add crumbled feta, spiking up the cold soup's flavor with pickled chiles and capers. In other words, my salmorejo is not far from a liquid version of Paximadi Salad (page 95). But let's start with the original recipe. If vine-ripened tomatoes are not available, a combination of regular tomatoes and some home-preserved ones works very well.

Makes 6 or more servings

2 pounds ripe but firm summer tomatoes (see Notes, page 95) or a combination of fresh and baked or half-cooked tomatoes (see page 212)

3 to 4 cups stale whole wheat bread cubes, preferably from sourdough, crusts removed

1 or 2 garlic cloves, peeled, to taste

2 tablespoons drained capers (optional)

3 or 4 small pickled chiles, or to taste

1 to 2 teaspoons sherry vinegar

$^1/_3$ cup extra virgin olive oil

Sea salt and freshly ground black pepper

TOPPINGS (use any or all)

$^1/_2$ cup Iberian ham or prosciutto in strips

2 hard-boiled eggs, chopped

1 cup crumbled feta cheese

Halve the tomatoes and put in a food processor or blender with 3 cups of the bread, the garlic, the capers if you're using them, the chiles, and 1 teaspoon of the vinegar. Process to make a smooth, thick mixture. With the machine running, add the olive oil. If the mixture seems too watery, add more bread. Taste and add more vinegar, plus salt and pepper to taste (the capers are quite salty, so you may not need additional salt if you used them).

Refrigerate overnight, preferably for 24 hours. The soup will thicken. Add some cold water to thin it if necessary and serve in bowls, sprinkling with one or more of the toppings if you like.

MAIN
COURSES

MOST COUNTRIES IN THE MEDITERRANEAN DON'T SHARE THE
Western notion of three-course meals. Dishes are rarely plated; they
are usually presented family style in the middle of the table, on large
platters, or served buffet style. At times foods will be offered in an
order Europeans and Americans might find incomprehensible. For
example, on Kea—the Greek island of the Cyclades where I live—a plate
of skillet-fried pork morsels is served at the very end of the dinner, even
after dessert.

I have tried to simplify things, calling all pastas "main courses" even
though Italians traditionally serve a small plate of pasta before the
main dish. You will find in this chapter recipes for one-pot meals, with
or without meat or fish, rice and grain pilafs, and of course beans and
chickpeas. You will also find stuffed vegetables, grilled or fried fish and
seafood, pies and tarts. After much thought, I decided to include as
main courses the hearty North African meatless soup with capers
(page 174), the lahmaçun (spicy meat-topped Arab pizza, page 118),
the glazed chicken wings (page 151), and the chakchouka (eggs
poached in pepper and tomato sauce, page 113). Some may think that
they are mezedes, and undoubtedly these dishes could be part of a
meze spread, but they certainly are too filling to be appetizers.

Grilled Calamari Stuffed with Olives, Almonds, and Pepper

Whenever we get good fresh calamari of any size, Costas, my husband, likes to stuff and grill it over charcoal or on the portable electric grill. He doesn't like the feta stuffing served with calamari at most Greek taverns, so he came up with this mixture of olives, almonds, and chiles. The calamari are very filling. Serve with just a green salad.

Makes 6 to 8 servings

8 to 10 medium-small calamari ($1^1/2$ to 2 pounds), cleaned, bone discarded, heads separated

MARINADE

3 tablespoons olive oil

2 tablespoons fresh lemon juice

Good pinch of Aleppo or Maraş pepper or hot red pepper flakes, to taste

STUFFING

3 tablespoons dried whole wheat bread crumbs or ground barley paximadi (see Sources)

$1/4$ cup raw almonds

$1/2$ cup firm green olives, pitted

Grated zest of 1 lemon, preferably organic

2 or 3 fresh thyme sprigs, chopped

$1^1/2$ to 3 teaspoons Aleppo or Maraş pepper, or a pinch of hot red pepper flakes, to taste

Sea salt

Wash the calamari inside and out and pat dry with paper towels. With scissors or a very sharp knife, cut a $1/4$-inch slit on one side, near the pointed end of each calamari tube.

In a bowl, mix the olive oil, lemon juice, and Aleppo pepper to make the marinade. Toss the calamari (body and heads) in the marinade, rubbing with your fingers and making sure they are moist inside and out. Set aside for about 20 minutes.

In a food processor or blender, pulse together the bread crumbs, almonds, olives, zest, thyme, and Aleppo pepper. Add salt sparingly since the olives are usually quite salty.

Light a charcoal grill, or heat a stove-top griddle.

Stuff each calamari tube with about 2 teaspoons stuffing and secure the top with a toothpick.

Place the stuffed calamari, cut side up, together with the heads on a well-oiled rack, close to the burning coals, or on a very hot oiled griddle. As the calamari tubes puff up, press carefully with tongs to extract the air. Grill until firm and marked, turning once or carefully rolling, to cook and mark on all sides, brushing every now and then with the marinade, about 8 minutes total. Slice and serve.

Grilled Calamari Stuffed with Olives, Almonds, and Pepper, page 101

Grilled Whole Fish in Chile,
Garlic, and Mint Sauce, page 104

✦ Grilled Whole Fish ✦
in Chile, Garlic, and Mint Sauce

In Jaffa, the picturesque old city next to Tel Aviv, Margaret Tayar has a famous seafood restaurant specializing in Moroccan cuisine prepared in her distinctive way. Her food—highly spiced and fragrant—is delicious. She is known for her fish couscous and for her simple and delicious spicy grilled fish. This recipe is my adaptation of Margaret's fresh and zesty salsa that dresses the charcoal-grilled bream. Serve with steamed potatoes, zucchini, and carrots. Makes 2 servings

2 to 4 fresh green chiles, minced, to taste

1 or 2 garlic cloves, minced, to taste

1 teaspoon dried mint, crumbled, or 3 tablespoons chopped fresh mint leaves

2 to 3 tablespoons fresh lemon juice, to taste

4 to 5 tablespoons fruity extra virgin olive oil, to taste

Sea salt and freshly ground black pepper

1 whole sea bream, porgy, or gray mullet (about $1^1/2$ pounds) or any other head-on fish, suitable for grilling, cleaned

$1/2$ cup finely diced peeled and seeded ripe fresh tomato, drained

2 tablespoons chopped fresh flat-leaf parsley

Mix together the chiles, garlic, mint, lemon juice, and olive oil in a bowl. Add a little salt and mix thoroughly, then taste and adjust the seasonings. The sauce should be hot. Let stand at room temperature for at least 30 minutes and up to 2 hours.

Light a charcoal grill or preheat the broiler.

Salt the fish inside and out and place on a well-oiled grill about 5 inches from the heat. Broil or grill, turning once, until firm and almost done, about 15 minutes total. Remove from the heat and cover with aluminum foil. Let stand for 5 minutes.

Mix the sauce with the chopped tomato. Serve the fish with the sauce on the side or cut the fish open, remove the central bone, and transfer the fillets to a heatproof platter. Pour half the sauce over the fish, sprinkle with some pepper, and place under a very hot broiler for a few seconds before serving, sprinkled with parsley. Pass the rest of the sauce separately.

✦ Grilled Tuna Marinated in Chermoula ✦

The boldly flavored Moroccan herb and spice marinade called *chermoula* is excellent with oily fish such as tuna or salmon, as well as with shrimp. You can marinate meat and poultry in it, and you can also serve chermoula as sauce for grilled or fried eggplant, zucchini, and other vegetables.

Serve the grilled tuna with steamed potatoes or a mixture of steamed vegetables—zucchini, carrots, green beans, broccoli, cauliflower—dressed in a simple lemon vinaigrette. Makes 4 servings

4 tuna steaks, about $^1/2$ inch thick

Sea salt

Chermoula (page 70)

A few fresh flat-leaf parsley sprigs and lemon slices for garnish

Wash the fish steaks and pat dry with paper towels. Salt them lightly. Rub the fish steaks on both sides with the chermoula and let stand for about 1 hour, covered, in the refrigerator.

Light a charcoal grill or preheat the broiler.

Grill or broil the tuna about 4 inches from the heat for 3 to 4 minutes on each side.

Garnish with sprigs of parsley and slices of lemon and serve.

✦ Fish Couscous ✦

Inspired by the unique Sicilian fish couscous, from Mary Taylor Simeti's wonderful book *Pomp and Sustenance*, I added a few more spices that bring the dish closer to its North African origins. You can make the broth a day in advance and finish the couscous the next day. Or you can even use good-quality bottled clam juice or frozen fish stock if you don't have time to prepare it from scratch. Packages of presteamed couscous advise just to moisten the grain with hot broth, but the result is better if you steam it once, as I describe here. Old-fashioned North African (not precooked) and barley couscous take longer to steam, but the grains are absolutely delicious. Makes 6 to 8 servings

About 3$^1/2$ pounds fish for soup (rockfish, grouper, John Dory, flounder, etc.), filleted, heads, tails, and bones reserved

BROTH AND VEGETABLES

2 or 3 medium carrots, halved lengthwise

2 onions, halved

4 fresh leaf celery (see Note, page 69) or common celery sprigs

5 fresh flat-leaf parsley sprigs

2 ripe fresh tomatoes, halved, or 1 cup good-quality canned tomatoes with their juice

2 to 4 dried peperoncini or chiles de árbol, halved lengthwise with scissors but left attached at the stem

Sea salt

COUSCOUS

1$^1/2$ cups Moroccan couscous or barley couscous (see Note)

1 cup olive oil

3 teaspoons Harissa (page 19), Hrous (page 29), or chile paste, mixed with $^1/4$ cup water, plus extra for the sauce

2 garlic cloves, minced

6 Turkish bay leaves

FISH FILLETS

Pinch of saffron threads, crumbled

$^1/2$ teaspoon ground turmeric

$^1/2$ teaspoon ground ginger

2 teaspoons ground cumin

Freshly ground black pepper

3 tablespoons olive oil

3 garlic cloves, minced

Place the fish heads, tails, bones, and other scraps in a pot with the carrots, onions, celery, parsley, tomatoes, dried chiles, and a pinch of salt. Add about 2 quarts cold water to cover, and bring to a boil. Boil over medium heat until the vegetables are tender and the fish falls from the bones, 30 minutes or more. Pass the broth through a fine strainer and discard the bones, tomato skins, chiles, parsley, and celery. (You can prepare the broth one day in advance. Keep the vegetables and bits of fish in the broth. Cool and refrigerate.)

Place the couscous in a bowl and mix with the oil, harissa, and garlic. Rub with your fingers to break the lumps and lubricate the grains. Line a coussoussière or a steamer with the bay leaves and add the couscous grains. Remove the vegetables and bits of fish from the broth and set aside. You must have about 5 cups broth. If less, add water. Bring the broth to a boil, lower the heat to simmer, and place the couscous on top. Steam the couscous, covered, for 20 minutes.

Meanwhile, mix together the saffron, turmeric, ginger, cumin, and black pepper with 1 teaspoon of the olive oil. Rub the fish fillets with the mixture, cover, and set aside for about 20 minutes. Heat the rest of the olive oil and sauté the garlic for 1 to 2 minutes, until it starts to color.

Remove the steamer from the pot and add the sautéed garlic and the fish fillets to the broth. Replace the steamer on top of the pot, increase the heat to medium, and cook the fish for 6 to 8 minutes, until firm, continuing to steam the couscous on top.

Remove the steamer and transfer the couscous to a large bowl or deep platter, arranging the bay leaves around the edge as decoration. Add 2 cups of the broth to the couscous and toss. Cover with foil and let stand for about 15 minutes. Slice the carrots and onion and add to the remaining broth with the fish. Heat through, remove from the heat, taste, and adjust the seasoning. In a separate bowl, mix $1/2$ cup of the broth with 3 to 4 teaspoons harissa to make the hot sauce.

Uncover the couscous and carefully fluff with a fork. Place the fish and vegetables on top of the couscous and moisten with whatever broth remains. Serve the fish couscous immediately, presenting the bowl with the hot sauce on the side, so that guests can spice up their couscous.

Note

Moroccan couscous (not precooked) and barley couscous (see Sources) need to be steamed three times. Prepare as directed, steam once, let rest, covered, for 10 minutes, moisten with about $2/3$ cup broth, steam again for 10 to 15 minutes, and let rest, uncovered, for about 10 minutes. Before the final steaming, moisten with about $2/3$ cup broth or water and steam once more.

✦ Fried Calamari Rings in Spicy Coating ✦

I remember the very tasty calamari I used to love to eat during our summer vacations in the Greek islands when I was a child. Today most of the calamari served in Greek tavernas and seaside restaurants is frozen, imported from faraway seas. Most of the calamari we now buy fresh or frozen has little flavor, so I have developed this spicy coating, which gives calamari a delightful flavor and crunchiness. Makes 3 to 4 servings

1 pound calamari, cleaned and cut into
$^1/_4$-inch rings

$^1/_4$ cup yellow cornmeal

$^1/_4$ cup stale whole wheat bread crumbs

3 tablespoons ground almonds

3 to 6 tablespoons Aleppo or Maraş pepper,
   or 2 to 3 pinches of hot red pepper flakes,
   to taste

$1^1/_2$ teaspoons dried oregano, thyme, or
   Za'atar (page 14)

Olive and sunflower oil (half and half) for
   deep-frying

1 egg

1 egg white

Sea salt

2 tablespoons milk

Lemon wedges for serving

Rinse the calamari rings. Mix the cornmeal, bread crumbs, almonds, Aleppo pepper, and oregano in a plastic bag. Add the moist calamari rings and shake in the bag until they are covered with the coating.

Heat about $1^1/2$ inches oil to 350°F in a deep skillet.

Beat the egg and egg white with some salt and the milk. Remove the coated calamari rings from the bag one at a time with tongs, dip in the egg mixture, and deep-fry in the hot oil until golden brown, 2 to 3 minutes. Do not crowd the pan, because the temperature of the oil will drop and you will end up with soggy calamari.

Transfer to a dish lined with double layers of paper towels. Sprinkle with salt and serve very hot with the lemon wedges.

Tuna or Swordfish with Wine, Vinegar, Tomato, Chile, and Capers

Tuna and swordfish have been caught using special nets or harpoons in the Mediterranean since ancient times. The population of these meaty fish is diminishing dramatically because of overfishing. Until a few years ago they were among the few affordable fish, considered second class, roughly in the same category as mackerel, sardines, and anchovies. Mediterranean cooks regard rich sliced tuna and swordfish as meat and often overcook it in rich sauces, making it dry and tasteless. Old recipes call for tuna steaks to be simmered for 30 or 40 minutes or baked for about 45 minutes.

The current demand for tuna in Japan and North America changed the way Mediterraneans view the fish. This Calabrian-inspired recipe is easy and fresh tasting. You can make it even faster using the All-Purpose Greek Tomato Sauce (page 22) if you have it on hand, adding chile, capers, and vinegar to taste. Serve with crusty bread for sopping up the wonderful juices. The fish steaks and sauce can also be served on top of freshly cooked spaghetti or linguine tossed with olive oil. Makes 4 servings

Olive oil

2 cups chopped onion

Sea salt

$1/2$ cup dry white wine

2 tablespoons red wine vinegar, or more to taste

1 to 3 dried peperoncini or chiles de árbol, thinly sliced with scissors, to taste

2 cups chopped or grated ripe fresh tomato (see page 212) or good-quality canned tomatoes with their juice

$1/4$ cup capers, preferably salt-packed, rinsed well and drained

$1/2$ to 1 teaspoon honey or sugar, to taste

4 tuna or swordfish steaks, 6 to 7 ounces each

$1/2$ teaspoon freshly ground black pepper, mixed with 1 teaspoon ground coriander seeds

2 tablespoons chopped fresh flat-leaf parsley

Heat 3 to 4 tablespoons olive oil in a large skillet over medium-high heat. Add the onion, sprinkle with salt, and sauté, stirring often, until soft and light golden, about 10 minutes. Add the wine, vinegar, and peperoncini and toss for 30 seconds. Pour in the tomatoes and cook for 5 minutes. Add the capers and $1/2$ teaspoon honey and cook for another 8 to 10 minutes, until the sauce thickens. Taste and adjust the flavor with more chile, vinegar, or honey. It should be quite intense—more or less sour, according to your taste. Transfer the sauce to a bowl and wipe the skillet with paper towels.

Heat 3 tablespoons olive oil in the skillet over medium-high heat. Sprinkle the fish steaks with salt and rub with the pepper-coriander mixture. Add to the hot skillet and sauté for 2 to 3 minutes on each side, until firm but still almost raw in the center. Add the sauce, bring to a boil, and cook for about 5 minutes, or until the fish is firm and just cooked through. Let the fish and sauce cool for 15 minutes or longer, then sprinkle with parsley and serve warm or at room temperature.

✦ Eggplants Stuffed with Bulgur and Meat ✦

In the colorful markets of southern Turkey one finds all sorts of dried vegetables next to dried peppers of various sizes. Dried purple-black hollowed eggplant halves are sold threaded on a string, like a strange oversized necklace. When eggplants were available only in the summer, this was the way for the eggplant-adoring Turks to enjoy them all year. In her wonderful book of historic Ottoman recipes, Marianna Gerasimos writes that she found the oldest recipe for stuffed eggplants in a 1764 cooking ledger. The recipe was entitled *Şeyhül mûhşi,* which means "Sheik of Stuffed Vegetables" or "Stuffed Vegetable for Sheiks," explains Gerasimos. In that old recipe the eggplant is stuffed with just ground lamb, garlic, and onions. The recipe that follows is my interpretation from a Gaziantep dish. I wish we could all get dried eggplant cups ready to stuff. It would make preparing this wonderful *bulgurlu patlican dolmasi* so much easier! I suggest you make the dish one or two days in advance. It tastes much better the next day.

Makes 6 to 8 servings

9 (6- to 7-inch-long) eggplants (about 3 pounds)

Sea salt and freshly ground black pepper

2 cups chopped onion

2 garlic cloves, chopped

$2/3$ pound ground lamb or beef

$1^1/2$ cups coarse bulgur (see Variation)

$1/2$ cup olive oil

1 tablespoon tomato paste

1 to 3 tablespoons chile paste, preferably Turkish, or Harissa (page 19), or a pinch of hot red pepper flakes, to taste

1 teaspoon sumac (optional)

1 teaspoon Baharat (page 12) or ground cumin plus a pinch of ground allspice

6 cups All-Purpose Greek Tomato Sauce (page 22)

1 cup chicken or vegetable stock, or more to taste

2 or 3 fresh flat-leaf parsley sprigs for garnish

Cut the eggplants in half crosswise and hollow each half carefully with a grapefruit spoon, taking out the inner flesh and leaving about $1/4$-inch-thick eggplant cups. Salt them inside and out and let them drain in a colander for about 30 minutes. Set aside the eggplant flesh for another dish, such as in the topping for Arab pizza (page 118).

In a bowl, mix the onion, garlic, meat,

bulgur, $^1/_4$ cup olive oil, tomato paste, chile paste, and sumac if you're using it. Add salt and pepper to taste and the baharat and stir thoroughly or, even better, knead with your hands to mix well.

Briefly rinse the eggplant cups and dry with paper towels. Stuff with the meat and bulgur mixture, leaving some room at the top for the stuffing to expand.

Warm $^1/_4$ cup olive oil in a large skillet or sauté pan over medium-high heat and sauté the stuffed eggplants, in batches if necessary, turning them carefully to brown on all sides. Don't worry; the stuffing won't run out. Pack all the eggplant cups back in the skillet, pour the tomato sauce over them, and add the stock. Liquid must come two-thirds of the way up the eggplant cups. Cook, covered, occasionally turning the eggplants, for 20 to 30 minutes, until tender and the stuffing is cooked.

Transfer the eggplants to a serving dish with a slotted spoon. If you have time, cool and refrigerate the eggplants and cooking liquid separately overnight. Just before serving, slice the cooled stuffed eggplants and reheat slowly in their sauce. Transfer to a serving dish, and if the sauce is too watery, increase the heat and cook for a few minutes to thicken. Pour the sauce over the eggplants, garnish with parsley, and serve.

VARIATION
Instead of bulgur, you can use trahana (page 42). Soak in cold water for 30 minutes, drain, and reserve the soaking liquid to add to the eggplants together with the tomato sauce. Mix the soaked trahana with the ground meat as directed.

Eggs Poached in Tomato and Chile Sauce

This dish is usually served as an appetizer in the Middle East, but it is quite filling, and I prefer to serve it as a main course for lunch or dinner. Similar to huevos rancheros, *chakchouka* gets its delicious flavor from the hot and fragrant chiles of the Mediterranean. The best chakchouka I've tasted was served in a restaurant called Doctor Chakchouka, in Jaffa, Israel. The owner served the dish in the skillet in which it was cooked, and diners dipped big pieces of crusty bread into it, devouring them instantly.

Makes 6 servings

3 tablespoons olive oil

1 cup chopped onion

2 green bell peppers, cut into strips

2 poblano chiles or red bell peppers, cut into strips

4 jalapeño chiles, seeded and cut into strips

2 cups grated ripe fresh tomatoes (see page 212) or good-quality canned chopped tomatoes with their juice

2 to 4 teaspoons Aleppo or Maraş pepper, or a pinch of hot red pepper flakes, to taste

Sea salt and freshly ground black pepper (optional)

6 eggs

Warm the olive oil in a large heavy skillet over medium-high heat. Add the onion, peppers, and chiles and sauté until soft, about 6 minutes, stirring with a wooden spatula. Add the tomatoes and cook until the mixture just starts to thicken, 8 to 10 minutes. Add the Aleppo pepper and some salt, taste, and adjust the seasoning.

Break one egg at a time into a cup or small bowl and slide it into the skillet while the tomato and pepper mixture is simmering. Cook for another 8 minutes, spooning sauce over the egg whites if you like until they are set. Sprinkle with Aleppo pepper and/or freshly ground black pepper and serve.

Swordfish with Wine, Vinegar,
Tomato, Chile, and Capers, page 109

Eggplants Stuffed with
Bulgur and Meat, page 111

Eggs Poached in Tomato and
Chile Sauce, page 113

Arab Pizza, page 118

Arab Pizza

I first tasted this delicious dish in a Turkish restaurant in Athens and later found it as street food in Egypt, Israel, and Turkey. Armenians call it "Armenian pizza." Claudia Roden, an expert on Middle Eastern food, told me that the dish originated in Egypt, where it is called *lahma bi ajeen*. In Turkey it is called *pide* or *lahmaçun* (pronounced lakh-mah-TZOON), the name used most commonly throughout the Mediterranean today.

The filling is spicy ground meat—originally lamb. I add some smoky eggplant, which enriches the lean meat I use. Arab Pizza can be made round or oval, like the ones I tried at a market bakery in Izmir. I prefer this shape because it can be folded more easily. In Izmir, a fiery red chile was baked on top. You can cut the pizza into pieces and serve it as an appetizer or serve it whole, as a main course, accompanied with Ezme Salatasi (page 84), a simple green salad, or Missir (macerated salad, page 83). If you don't want to make your own bread dough, slice a commercial whole wheat pita horizontally and use each half as a base for the filling. Makes 8 small pizzas

DOUGH

1 teaspoon active dry yeast

1 cup whole wheat flour

2 to 2$^1/2$ cups all-purpose flour, or 1 cup all-purpose plus 1$^1/2$ cups bread flour

3 tablespoons olive oil

1$^1/2$ cups warm water, or more if needed

1 teaspoon coarse sea salt

FILLING

$^1/3$ cup olive oil

2 cups chopped onion

1 medium eggplant, finely diced, salted, and left to drain in a colander for 30 minutes

1 medium green bell pepper, diced

1 medium red bell pepper, diced

1 tablespoon tomato paste

1 to 2 tablespoons Aleppo or Maraş pepper, or a pinch of hot red pepper flakes, to taste

1 pound lean ground beef, turkey, or chicken

1$^1/2$ cups grated ripe fresh tomatoes (see page 212) or drained good-quality canned diced tomatoes

$^1/2$ teaspoon ground allspice and/or $^1/2$ to 1 teaspoon Ras el Hanout (page 13)

Sea salt

$^1/2$ cup finely chopped fresh flat-leaf parsley

$^1/3$ cup pine nuts (optional)

8 small fresh red chiles for topping the pizzas

Put the yeast and flours in the bowl of a stand mixer filled with the dough hook. Mix for a few seconds to combine. Add the olive oil and half the water and mix for about 2 minutes. Add the salt and more water and mix for another 2 to 3 minutes. The dough should be soft and slightly sticky.

Turn the dough out onto a lightly floured board and knead with lightly oiled hands until the dough is no longer sticky. Form into a ball, oil the bottom of a large bowl, and roll the dough into it. Cover with oiled plastic wrap and let rise in a warm place for about $1^1/2$ hours, until doubled. (You can also leave the dough overnight in the refrigerator. The next day, leave it at room temperature for about 2 hours before proceeding.)

To make the filling, warm 3 tablespoons of the olive oil in a skillet over medium-high heat, add the onion, and sauté until translucent, about 3 minutes. Rinse the diced eggplant under cold water, pat dry with paper towels, and add to the skillet along with the bell peppers. Sauté, stirring often, until all the vegetables are wilted, 6 to 8 minutes. Add the tomato paste and toss for a minute, then add 1 tablespoon of the Aleppo pepper and the ground meat. Sauté, stirring, until the meat is no longer red. Add the tomato pulp, allspice and/or ras el hanout, and salt to taste. Toss until almost all the juices have evaporated, 8 to 10 minutes. Remove from the heat, add the parsley, taste, and adjust the seasoning. The filling should have a strong flavor.

Warm the rest of the olive oil with 2 to 3 teaspoons more Aleppo pepper and set aside. Place a pizza stone or a large heavy baking sheet in the oven. Preheat the oven to 450°F.

On a lightly floured board, divide the risen dough into 8 pieces and flatten each one of them with your palm. Cut an 8 X 20-inch piece of parchment paper and roll out each piece of dough on it with a floured rolling pin to form an elongated oval about 5 X 12 inches. Brush the flattened dough with the peppered oil and then spread about $1/2$ cup of the filling evenly on each pizza, covering the entire surface, as is the custom in the Middle East, or leaving a border uncovered if you like. Sprinkle with the pine nuts if you're using them, and place one chile on each pizza.

Put on the heated stone or pan as many pizzas as it can hold, sliding them in with the parchment paper. Bake for 15 to 20 minutes, until the filling sizzles and the crust is golden brown. Keep the baked pizzas warm as you bake the rest. Cut each pizza in two, if you like, and fold lengthwise. Wrap half in parchment paper and serve warm or at room temperature as finger food.

Calabrian Tomato Tart

The crust of this peasant tart contains wine, eggs, lard, and grated pecorino cheese. The crunchy biscuitlike shell is topped with fresh tomatoes and chiles, creating a delicious and unusual "pitta." It can be eaten warm or at room temperature and is ideal for a summer buffet lunch or dinner. *Pizzulata,* in the Calabrian dialect, means "pinched with the fingertips" (*pizzicotare* in Italian), describing the way the dough is spread on the baking sheet. I use halved cherry tomatoes for a more attractive tart, but regular sliced tomatoes work fine. Makes 4 servings

CRUST

$2^1/2$ cups all-purpose flour, or $1^1/2$ cups all-purpose plus 1 cup whole wheat flour

$1^1/2$ cups grated pecorino Romano cheese

$1/2$ to 1 teaspoon freshly ground black pepper, to taste

4 ounces lard or a combination of olive oil and lard or unsalted butter (about $1/2$ cup total)

$1/4$ cup dry white wine, or more as needed

2 eggs, lightly beaten

TOPPING

About $2/3$ pound cherry tomatoes (not the very tiny ones) or sliced ripe but firm tomatoes

2 or 3 jalapeño chiles or 1 or 2 fresh Anaheim chiles, to taste, seeded and thinly sliced

Fleur de sel or other finishing salt

Pulse all the crust ingredients except 2 tablespoons of the beaten eggs in a food processor. Work the mixture very briefly, adding 1 or 2 tablespoons wine or water if needed to make a soft sticky dough. Cover with plastic wrap and let stand for 30 minutes.

Preheat the oven to 375°F. Line an 11 X 14-inch baking sheet with parchment paper.

Transfer the dough to the pan, stretching it and pressing with wet fingers to make a rectangle about 11 X 14 inches. Brush the top with the reserved egg. Cut each cherry tomato in half horizontally and arrange the pieces over the dough, alternating cut side up and cut side down. Scatter the chopped chiles around the tomatoes, pressing carefully on the tomatoes and chiles so they stick to the dough. Sprinkle with salt and bake for 35 to 40 minutes, or until the crust is golden brown and the tomatoes wrinkled, with a few black spots.

Let cool on a rack and cut into pieces to serve warm or at room temperature.

◆ Calabrian Pita ◆

he covered pizzas of Calabria—called *pita*—are the perfect example of a hearty rustic
food that I never tire of. Besides being delicious, Calabrian pitas have particular
significance for me. First because the word *pita*—which has come to mean "flat bread" all
over the world—in modern Greek also means "covered pie," and I find it very moving that
the same word is used in Calabria. Second, I love the breadlike dough that encases the
filling because even by itself it is flavorful and doesn't require the dexterity needed to roll
the paper-thin phyllo sheets of the traditional Greek pita. I am not fond of commercial
frozen phyllo, as it has no flavor. The basic idea behind pita and pizza, both dishes with
ancient roots, is a well-balanced combination of crust and flavorings or filling. The spicy
stuffing of Calabrian pita wonderfully complements the thin bread that encases it.

I love making bread, and I can start a dough at any moment. But I know that many
people aren't eager to try making a yeasted crust, so I give the recipe for a faster version
with baking powder. The texture is not the same, but it works fine, as does good store-
bought pizza dough.

Pita with Tuna, Olives, Capers, and Peperoncini

Makes 8 to 10 servings

YEASTED CRUST
(see also Notes and Variation)

2 teaspoons active dry yeast

$3^1/2$ to 4 cups all-purpose flour, or $1^1/2$ cups
whole wheat plus 2 cups or more all-
purpose flour

1 tablespoon coarse sea salt or kosher salt

$1/2$ cup olive oil

FILLING

2 tablespoons olive oil

Two $1/2$-inch-thick slices pancetta, cut into
thin strips, or $1^1/2$ tablespoons pork fat

3 large garlic cloves, thinly sliced

3 to 4 dried peperoncini, slashed in half from
stem to tip or finely cut with scissors

4 anchovy fillets or salted sardines (see
Notes), chopped

1 pound ripe fresh summer tomatoes, grated
(see page 212) or one 16-ounce can good-
quality, chopped tomatoes with their juice

(continued)

2 to 3 tablespoons capers, preferably salt-packed, rinsed well and drained

1/2 cup juicy black olives, pitted and coarsely chopped

Two 6-ounce cans good-quality tuna in olive oil, drained

Sea salt and Aleppo pepper or hot red pepper flakes, to taste

2 eggs, lightly beaten

2 to 3 tablespoons milk for brushing the pita (optional)

Combine the yeast and 1 cup cold water in a food processor and pulse to blend. Working at low speed, add 3^1/2 cups of the flour, the salt, and the olive oil and process until well combined. If the dough is too wet, add a little more flour; if it is too dry, add 1 to 2 tablespoons water. Lightly oil a large bowl and a piece of plastic wrap. Place the dough in the bowl, cover with the oiled plastic wrap, and let rise until almost doubled in volume, 45 to 60 minutes.

Meanwhile, make the filling: Heat the olive oil in a large skillet over medium heat. Add the pancetta, garlic, and peperoncini and cook, stirring, for 3 to 4 minutes, until the garlic starts to color. Add the anchovies and tomatoes and cook, stirring every now and then, for 10 minutes or more, until the sauce thickens. Add the capers and olives and cook for another 2 to 3 minutes. The sauce should be quite thick. Stir in the tuna and remove from the heat. Taste and add salt and Aleppo pepper. The filling should

have a strong flavor. Let cool and stir in the eggs.

Turn the dough out onto a lightly floured surface and cut in two, with one piece considerably larger than the other. Oil a 15-inch pizza pan. Flatten and stretch the larger piece of dough to cover the bottom of the pan with about 1 inch of overhang. Wet your fingers as you push and shape the dough. Spread the filling evenly on the surface of the crust inside the pan. Roll the second piece of dough with a rolling pin to make a disk that will just cover the pan and place it over the filling. Wet the edge all around and fold the overhanging bottom crust inward. Pinch the edges together, making a neat cord around the edge of the pan. Flatten the cord with your finger or the tines of a fork to prevent it from sticking out, or it will burn during baking. Let stand for 20 minutes.

Preheat the oven to 450°F.

Prick the surface of the pita with a skewer and, if you like, brush with milk. Bake on the floor of the oven for 10 minutes. Lower the oven temperature to 400°F and bake for 35 minutes or more, until golden brown on top. Cover loosely with aluminum foil and bake for another 10 minutes. Lift carefully with a large spatula and check to make sure the bottom is well browned. If not, bake for a few more minutes. Transfer to a rack to cool for about 15 minutes before cutting into wedges to serve.

Notes

The dough for Basic Bread with Spices (page 177), made with a combination of flours, can be used instead of this white flour yeasted crust. Just add olive oil.

Good Italian dry-salted sardines are the ones used in Calabria. They are much more flavorful than anchovies. If you can get them (see Sources), scrape out the salt with kitchen paper, briefly rinse under cold water, and pat dry with paper towels.

QUICK CRUST WITH BAKING POWDER

4 cups all-purpose flour

1 tablespoon baking powder

Pinch of sea salt

1/2 cup olive oil

In a large bowl, mix the flour with the baking powder and salt. Add the olive oil and rub the ingredients between your hands until the texture is like bread crumbs. Gradually add enough water, $2/3$ to 1 cup, to make a soft, elastic dough. Cover with plastic wrap and let rest for 2 to 3 minutes. Alternatively, you can make the dough in a food processor. Combine the dry ingredients and pulse to mix. Then, with the motor running, add the liquids. Let the dough rest for 3 to 5 minutes. Divide and proceed as for the yeasted dough.

Pita with Spicy Calabrian Sausage

Well-seasoned Calabrian sausages—like the ones called *diavoletti*—are used as stuffing for pita. Loose spicy sausage meat is sold in jars in Calabria, and it is ideal for this covered pizza.

Makes 8 to 10 servings

Yeasted Crust or Quick Crust with Baking Powder (preceding recipe) or Basic Bread with Spices (page 177)

1 pound spicy sausage—Spanish or Mexican chorizo or a combination of Italian sausage and chorizo

Hot red pepper flakes or Aleppo pepper

Prepare the crust, divide, and lay in the pan as described in the preceding recipe.

To make the filling, slit the sausage and remove the casing. Chop the filling. Heat a skillet over medium-high heat and cook the sausage meat in it for 10 to 15 minutes, stirring often, until firm. Remove with a slotted spoon and arrange on the dough. Drizzle with a little of the fat from the pan and sprinkle with some water. Add pepper to taste. Cover with the rest of the dough as described in the preceding recipe. Brush with some of the skillet fat and bake until well browned on the top and bottom (see the preceding recipe).

✦ Spicy, Light Moussaka ✦

This is the version of the ever-popular dish that I cook at home. Moussaka, although the most well-known Greek dish, is in fact not a traditional recipe but a Middle Eastern one. There are numerous variations throughout the region. The basic Arab *mousaquaa* consists of fried eggplant slices topped with spicy tomato sauce and is served cold. In the 1920s, Tselementes, a talented Greek chef, invented moussaka as we know it today. My meatless variation is closer to the original Middle Eastern dish. My mother called her meatless version *pseudo-moussaka* and often cooked it in a large pan for summer parties. Both versions are ideal for parties, and you can easily double or triple the recipe. Prepare it one day in advance, let it cool, refrigerate, and reheat (only the one with meat) just before serving. Moussaka tastes better the next day, when all the flavors have had time to blend. Makes 6 servings as a main course, 8 to 10 as part of a buffet

Sea salt

2 large eggplants (about 1^1/2 pounds), sliced lengthwise ^{1}/4 inch thick

Olive oil

1 pound potatoes, peeled and sliced ^{1}/4 inch thick

3 large green bell peppers, quartered lengthwise and cut into 1-inch pieces

1 pound lean ground lamb

1^1/2 cups chopped onion

3 to 5 teaspoons Aleppo or Maraş pepper, or 1 or 2 pinches of cayenne, or to taste

^{1}/3 cup dry red wine

^{1}/2 cup dried currants

1 pound ripe fresh red tomatoes, grated (see page 212), or 2^1/2 cups good-quality canned chopped tomatoes with their juice

5 or 6 grindings of black pepper, or to taste

1 or 2 pinches of freshly grated nutmeg

1 teaspoon Ras el Hanout (page 13), or a good pinch of ground allspice

1 pound (4 cups) Greek yogurt, preferably sheep's milk (see page 213), or a combination of 2 parts yogurt and 1 part heavy cream

2 egg yolks

Salt the eggplant slices, place them in a colander, and let them drain for at least 30 minutes. Meanwhile, heat about 1 inch of olive oil in a deep, heavy skillet over medium-high heat and briefly fry the potato slices without letting them cook through. Remove with a slotted spoon and layer them on the bottom of a 9 X 12-inch glass or ceramic ovenproof dish at least 2^1/2 inches deep (or an equivalent round or oval dish).

In the same frying oil, sauté the peppers over medium-high heat, stirring often, until they start to color, about 10 minutes. Remove with a slotted spoon and reserve. Reserve the frying oil, measure out $^1/_2$ cup, and return it to the pan. Sauté the lamb in the oil, stirring often, for about 10 minutes, until no longer red. Add the chopped onion and continue to sauté, stirring, for another 10 minutes, or until the onion becomes translucent. Add the Aleppo pepper and the red wine. When the mixture boils, add the currants and tomatoes. Lower the heat and simmer for about 15 minutes. Season to taste with salt and freshly ground black pepper, add the nutmeg and ras el hanout, and remove from the heat. The mixture should be thick and quite spicy.

Preheat the broiler.

Wipe the eggplant slices with paper towels and place them on a baking sheet. Brush both sides with the reserved oil and broil about 4 inches from the heat until golden on both sides.

Preheat the oven to 400°F.

Arrange the eggplant slices over the potatoes. It doesn't matter if they overlap somewhat. Layer the sautéed peppers over the eggplant and top with the lamb and tomato sauce. In a bowl, mix the yogurt with the egg yolks, stirring well. Pour the mixture over the lamb and tomato mixture. Bake for about 1 hour, until the top starts to color and the moussaka is bubbly. Let cool completely and refrigerate.

To reheat, place in a preheated oven at 375°F for about 20 minutes, until bubbly.

MEATLESS SPICY MOUSSAKA
Substitute $1^1/_2$ cups coarsely ground walnuts for the lamb, mixing them with the tomato sauce. Top with the yogurt-egg mixture or simply sprinkle the tomato-walnut sauce with $^1/_2$ cup dried bread crumbs and 1 cup coarsely grated hard feta cheese. Serve at room temperature.

Potato "Focaccia"

In the strong dialect of southern Italy, this hearty family dish is called *fucazza de petate,* as Tonio Piceci writes in his charming book *Oltre le Orecchiette* ("More than Ear-Shaped Pasta"), in which he has gathered recipes from the region of Salento, in Apulia. His version contains no *peperoncini*—the particularly hot small Italian chiles—but several cooks in the region told me that they add them to the fucazza. Others insisted that chile olive oil—*diauliciu* ("the devil's condiment")—is often drizzled over the dish before baking to give it an extra bite. Italian peperoncini come in various forms and sizes and have a marvelous flavor as well as heat. Chile de árbol and Aleppo or Maraş pepper make good substitutes. Makes 4 to 6 servings

3 pounds waxy potatoes, freshly boiled and mashed

1 cup grated pecorino Romano cheese

$1/2$ cup grated Parmesan cheese

5 tablespoons olive oil, plus oil for the dish

$2 1/2$ cups chopped onion

2 or 3 dried peperoncini or chiles de árbol, thinly sliced or snipped with scissors, 3 to 5 tablespoons Aleppo or Maraş pepper, or hot red pepper flakes, to taste

1 dried Turkish bay leaf (optional)

$1/3$ cup dry white wine

1 cup grated ripe fresh tomatoes (see page 212) or good-quality canned chopped tomatoes with their juice

3 tablespoons capers, preferably salt-packed, rinsed well and drained

$1/2$ cup chopped pitted small black Italian or Kalamata olives

Sea salt and freshly ground black pepper

Peperoncini sott'Olio (page 36) or plain olive oil

2 to 3 tablespoons toasted whole wheat or multigrain bread crumbs

In a bowl, mix the mashed potatoes with the cheeses, stirring vigorously. Warm the olive oil in a heavy skillet over medium-high heat, add the onion, and sauté for 5 minutes, until soft. Add the peperoncini, bay leaf if you're using it, and wine and stir a couple of times. Pour in the tomatoes and cook over medium heat for about 5 minutes. Add the capers and olives and cook for 5 minutes longer, until most of the liquid has evaporated. Discard the bay leaf, taste, and adjust the seasoning, adding salt and freshly ground black pepper.

Thoroughly oil a deep clay or glass oven-proof pie dish and preheat the oven to 375°F.

Divide the potato mixture in half and cover the bottom of the dish with one half. Pour the tomato mixture over the potato, spreading it evenly. Cover with the rest of the potato, pressing down well with your hands. Prick the surface with the tines of a fork, drizzle with Peperoncini sott'Olio or plain olive oil and some Aleppo or freshly ground pepper, and sprinkle with the bread crumbs. Bake for 40 to 45 minutes, until golden brown and bubbly. Serve hot or at room temperature.

Skillet Pork from Kea

In Kea and the other Cyclades, during the heart of the winter, when seaside taverns are closed and the cold northern wind vigorously beats the deserted beaches, islanders slaughter their pigs. Pig slaughtering is still an occasion to gather in this or that home and eat and drink homemade wine and raki (grappa) while helping divide the meat, make sausages, and prepare the much-valued *loza*—wine-marinated pork loin, which is spiced, inserted into the pork's large intestine, and smoked for two days.

Little trimmings of pork meat are cooked on the spot or saved for other occasions. They are briefly sautéed in the skillet with wine and sweet spices, to be enjoyed with bread and plenty of wine. The dish is called *tigania* (*tigani* is the skillet), and it is usually served as a late-night treat, on all sorts of occasions, after the meal and even after the sweets. During the long Kean dinners, in the wee hours of the morning, as diners continue to drink, sing, and dance, a tigania is whipped up. It is a tradition that I found extremely odd when I first encountered it, at a Kean wedding. A waiter brought the pieces of meat to our table after we had just finished our *galaktoboureko* (milk custard). The whole restaurant was reserved for the wedding, but it never occurred to me that tigania was deliberately served on top of our dessert after an unbelievably rich meal. So I gave it back to the waiter, protesting that it was some kind of mix-up and probably belonged to another table.

The first recipe is a more recent version with tomato and is based on the tigania my neighbor Zenobia Stefa prepares every so often. The second is the older and most common tigania served in island taverns. Since in my house we hardly ever have occasions for a late-night snack, I like to serve my tigania with tagliatelle or ziti, or with mashed potatoes, as a main course. Makes 4 to 6 servings

2 pounds boneless pork shoulder with some fat, cut into 1 1/2-inch cubes

Olive oil

Sea salt and freshly ground black pepper

1 tablespoon tomato paste

(continued)

$^1/2$ cup semisweet red wine, or $^1/4$ cup red wine plus $^1/4$ cup Greek Mavrodaphne or Marsala wine

1 cup good-quality canned chopped tomatoes with their juice

1 teaspoon black peppercorns

2 whole allspice

One 3-inch cinnamon stick

1 or 2 good pinches of Aleppo or Maraş pepper or a pinch of hot red pepper flakes, to taste (optional)

Fresh country bread to dip in the sauce or 1 pound tagliatelle or ziti, cooked and drizzled with olive oil, or mashed potatoes

If the meat is too fatty, discard some of the fat, leaving some so that the dish will have flavor. Wash the meat and pat dry.

In a deep skillet, warm 2 to 3 tablespoons of olive oil over medium-high heat. Add the meat and sauté until browned on all sides, about 8 minutes. Add salt and plenty of black pepper and stir. Add the tomato paste and sauté for 2 minutes longer, until the meat looks glossy. Add the wine and bring to a boil. Add the tomatoes.

In a mortar, briefly crush the peppercorns and allspice and add them to the meat along with the cinnamon and about $^1/2$ cup water, adding a little more water or wine if necessary to come two-thirds of the way up the meat. When the liquid starts to boil, lower the heat, cover, and simmer for about 20 minutes, or until the meat is tender.

If there is excessive liquid in the pan, uncover and boil over high heat to reduce. Discard the cinnamon stick, sprinkle with Maraş or Aleppo pepper if you like, and serve immediately, in the pan, with plenty of crusty bread and, of course, Greek wine.

If you serve with pasta, toss the cooked oiled pasta with the meat in a heated bowl. You can also refrigerate when cool. Before serving, warm the meat over low heat.

⋆ Tomatoless Tigania ⋆

Tomatoes were introduced to our part of the world via Italy and didn't become the ubiquitous ingredient they are today until the beginning of the twentieth century. So this winter version probably dates back to the time when tomatoes were nonexistent or considered exotic. Flavored with plenty of lemon juice and wild savory or oregano, the original tigania is irresistible and is best enjoyed with just crusty bread. Makes 6 servings

2 pounds boneless pork shoulder with some fat, cut into $1^1/2$-inch cubes

Olive oil

Sea salt and freshly ground black pepper

$^1/2$ cup dry white wine

3 to 4 tablespoons fresh lemon juice, or more to taste

1 teaspoon honey or sugar

1 teaspoon black peppercorns, lightly crushed

Large pinch of dried wild summer savory or dried Greek oregano

Fresh country bread for serving

Prepare the meat as in the preceding recipe. In a skillet, warm 2 to 3 tablespoons of olive oil over medium-high heat. Add the meat and sauté until browned on all sides, about 8 minutes. Add salt and pepper to taste and stir. Pour in the wine, lemon juice, and honey, and when the liquid starts to boil, add the crushed peppercorns and half the savory.

Add enough wine or water to almost cover the meat. When it starts to boil, lower the heat, cover, and simmer for about 20 minutes, until the meat is tender. If there is excessive liquid in the pan, uncover and boil over high heat to reduce. Taste and correct the seasoning, sprinkling with the remaining savory. Serve immediately, in the skillet, with plenty of crusty bread and Greek wine.

✦ Roasted Leg of Lamb ✦
with North African Spices, Lemon, and Onions

I call this herb and spice rub North African because, besides the classic oregano and rosemary, it contains Tunisian and Moroccan spices such as caraway, cumin, and turmeric. In addition, it is spiked with harissa, the ubiquitous hot pepper paste that is to Arab North Africa what chile oil is to Asia.

Use the same spice mixture to rub poultry, beef, or pork two to three hours before grilling and leave at room temperature. Or you can mix 3 tablespoons of this rub with 3 tablespoons yogurt and baste chicken breasts or legs or skewered lamb and pork before grilling. Better yet, leave in the spicy yogurt marinade in the refrigerator overnight.

Makes 6 servings

SPICE MIXTURE

3 tablespoons coarse sea salt

2 teaspoons dried Greek oregano or savory

1 teaspoon chopped fresh rosemary leaves

3 teaspoons caraway seeds

1 teaspoon cumin seeds

$^1/_2$ teaspoon ground turmeric

2 tablespoons Harissa (page 19) or Aleppo or
   Maraş pepper to taste

1 teaspoon chopped garlic, or 1 tablespoon
   Roasted Garlic Skordalia (page 51)

$^1/_4$ cup olive oil

One 5- to 6-pound bone-in leg of lamb

$^1/_4$ cup fresh lemon juice

$^1/_3$ cup dry white wine, or more if needed

$1^1/_2$ pounds medium or small red onions,
   peeled and halved or quartered

2 or 3 fresh rosemary sprigs, or 1 tablespoon
   dried

In a spice grinder, a clean coffee grinder, or a mortar, grind the salt, oregano, rosemary, caraway, cumin, and turmeric to a fine powder. Transfer to a bowl and add the harissa and chopped garlic. Add the olive oil to make a thick paste.

Make 8 or 9 deep slits all over the lamb and insert some of the spice paste, rubbing the paste all over the surface of the meat. Cover and let stand for 1 hour at room temperature or, preferably, refrigerate for at least 5 hours or overnight. Bring to room temperature before roasting.

Preheat the oven to 450°F.

Place the leg of lamb fat side down in a roasting pan that will hold the onions in one layer. Roast for 20 minutes. Mix the lemon juice and wine in a small bowl. Turn the meat and pour the lemon-wine mixture over it. (If you are roasting the lamb in a clay dish, warm the mixture first, because cold liquid can cause the clay to crack.) Reduce the oven temperature to 375°F and roast for 35 minutes, basting every 10 to 15 minutes with the pan juices. If the pan dries out, add a little more wine.

Transfer the lamb to a plate and add the onions to the pan, tossing them well to coat them with the pan juices. Add the rosemary sprigs or sprinkle with dried rosemary, toss, place the lamb on the onions, and continue roasting, basting often, for another 30 minutes, or until an instant-read thermometer inserted into the thickest part of the meat reads 135°F.

Transfer the meat to a heated platter, cover with a double layer of aluminum foil, and set aside. (Leave the oven on.) If the pan juices are watery, transfer most of them to a saucepan and cook briefly to reduce. Meanwhile, return the pan to the oven and continue baking the onions until tender, with browned edges. Turn the oven to broil. Place the lamb on the onions again and broil for 2 to 3 minutes, or until the surface is deep brown and crackling. Carve the lamb and serve, passing the pan juices in a bowl or sauceboat at the table.

✦ Slow-Baked Lamb with Wheat Berries ✦

During important religious festivals at some Greek village churches, women and men prepare a communal meal consisting of meat—usually lamb or goat—cut into pieces and cooked in large cauldrons over a makeshift charcoal fire, together with wheat berries. The kernals are often coarsely cracked in stone handmills (not to be confused with common bulgur, where the cracked wheat is presteamed and dried). The cooks take turns constantly stirring the contents of the cauldron with long wooden paddles for hours. The food is considered cooked when meat and wheat berries are almost reduced to a pulp.

In Samos this concoction is simply called *giorti* ("feast"), but in Lesbos and in parts of mainland Greece the dish is called *kiskek*. In Anatolia, in southern Turkey, *kashkek* is a similar festive dish. The word probably shares an ancient root with *kishke*, the traditional Jewish meat-and-grain sausage. Similar dishes have been cooked all over the Mediterranean for various communal celebrations since antiquity. The spices vary, following local traditions; tomatoes are the only "modern" addition to this simple age-old dish.

My recipe is a more contemporary take on the old *kiskek*. Oranges are often added to stews in the southern Peloponnese. I love wheat berries and think their bite and nutty, earthy flavor ideally complement the lamb in a combination that is more interesting than the common orzo *youvetsi*, to which this dish is closely related. Makes 6 to 8 servings

$^1/_3$ cup olive oil

6 lamb shanks, about $^3/_4$ pound each, halved crosswise by the butcher

2 large onions, sliced

Sea salt and freshly ground black pepper

1 tablespoon coriander seeds

1 tablespoon allspice seeds

4 Turkish bay leaves

One $2^1/_2$-inch 1 cinnamon stick

$2^1/_2$ cups semisweet rosé wine, such as white Zinfandel, or a mixture of white and red wine

2 whole oranges, preferably organic, halved and cut into $^1/_2$-inch slices

2 to 4 teaspoons Aleppo or Maraş pepper, or a pinch of hot red pepper flakes, to taste

$1^1/2$ cups grated ripe fresh tomatoes (see page 212) or good-quality canned chopped tomatoes with their juice

About 5 cups chicken or beef stock

$2^1/2$ cups wheat berries (see Sources), soaked in very warm water for 30 minutes

In a heavy Dutch oven, warm the olive oil over medium-high heat. Add the meat and sauté in batches on all sides until browned, about 15 minutes. Transfer the meat to a platter, cover, and set aside.

Preheat the oven to 375°F.

Add the onions to the oil, sprinkle with salt, and sauté for about 10 minutes, stirring often, until very soft. Coarsely crush the coriander and allspice in a mortar or with the back of a heavy knife. Cut a piece of cheesecloth (8 to 10 inches square), place the crushed spices in the center, and tie with kitchen twine. Add to the onions along with the bay leaves and cinnamon stick.

Return the meat to the pan and bring to a boil over medium heat. Add $1^1/2$ cups of the wine and the oranges. As the liquid starts to boil, add the Aleppo pepper, tomatoes, and 1 cup of the stock. Stir and bring to a boil. Then cover and transfer the meat to the oven. Bake for $1^1/2$ hours, turning the pieces often to keep them moist in the sauce. Add stock as needed to keep the meat half-covered. You can prepare the meat to this point up to 3 days in advance. Cool and refrigerate in the sauce.

Return the pot to the stove. Add the remaining 1 cup wine plus 3 cups stock, stir, and bring to a boil. Drain the soaked wheat berries and add to the meat, stir, cover, and transfer to the oven. Bake for about $1^1/2$ hours, or until meat and berries are cooked, adding stock as needed to keep the berries moist. Taste and add salt and pepper. Discard the cheesecloth with the spices and serve hot.

Slow-Baked Lamb
with Wheat
Berries, page 136

Braised Veal with Artichokes in
Egg and Lemon Sauce, page 140

✦ Braised Veal with Artichokes ✦ in Egg and Lemon Sauce

Avgolemono (egg and lemon sauce), the elegant creamy and tangy finish to meat and vegetable dishes, has its roots in the Sephardic *agristada*. It was probably introduced to Greece by the Jews of Andalusia, who fled the persecutions of Spain in the fifteenth century and settled in Salonika, Istanbul, and other cities around the Mediterranean. Agristada is used mostly with fish—poached or fried—in the Sephardic tradition (see the variation). Greeks use avgolemono to thicken meat and chicken soups and the cooking juices of meat-filled dolmades (stuffed cabbage or grape leaves). Lamb, veal, and pork stews braised with seasonal vegetables are often complemented with this versatile sauce. Mixed greens and leaf celery with its bulby root are the most common additions to the winter meat stews, while in the spring lamb or veal avgolemono with artichokes is one of the most revered dishes of Greek urban cuisine. Contrary to the mild dish my mother cooked, I add green chiles or plenty of freshly ground pepper to my veal and artichoke avgolemono. Makes 4 servings

$1/2$ cup olive oil

$1^1/2$ pounds boneless veal shank (or pork loin), cut into 2-inch cubes

Sea salt and freshly ground black pepper

1 cup sliced red or white onions

$1^1/2$ cups coarsely chopped scallion, including most of the green

1 to 3 jalapeño chiles, seeded and chopped, or freshly ground black or white pepper

1 cup dry white wine

$1^1/2$ cups chicken or beef stock

8 medium artichokes, trimmed and halved (see Note)

$1^1/2$ cups chopped fresh dill

EGG AND LEMON SAUCE (AVGOLEMONO)

2 large eggs

1 teaspoon cornstarch

$1/4$ cup plus 1 tablespoon fresh lemon juice, or more to taste

Sea salt and freshly ground black pepper or a good pinch of Aleppo or Maraş pepper to taste

Heat the oil in a large deep skillet or a Dutch oven over medium-high heat. Add the meat in batches and sauté, turning often, until golden on all sides, about 10 minutes. Season with salt and pepper. Add the onions, scallion, and jalapeños and sauté for 2 or 3 minutes more, or until soft. Add the wine and bring to a boil. Pour in the stock and bring back to a boil. Reduce the heat to low and simmer for 30 minutes.

Add the artichokes and a little water if needed—the liquid should almost cover the meat and artichokes. Place an inverted heatproof plate over the meat and artichokes to keep them submerged. Cook, uncovered, for about 20 minutes, or until the artichokes are tender and the meat is fully cooked.

With a slotted spoon, transfer the meat and artichokes to a platter. Add 1 cup of the dill and if the sauce is too thin, increase the heat to high and boil for 3 to 4 minutes to reduce. You should have 2 to $2^{1}/2$ cups of broth.

To make the avgolemono sauce, whisk the eggs with 2 tablespoons water in a medium bowl. Dissolve the cornstarch in the lemon juice and add to the egg mixture. Whisking constantly, and using a ladle, slowly pour about half the sauce from the pan into the eggs. Then slowly pour the egg mixture back into the pot with the cooking liquid, whisking constantly to prevent the eggs from curdling. As the sauce thickens, add the meat and artichokes to the pan, taste, and add lemon juice, salt, and/or black pepper or Aleppo pepper. Add the rest of the dill, reserving a tablespoon for serving, and simmer for 2 minutes more to warm through. Sprinkle with dill and pepper and serve.

Note
To prepare the artichokes, fill a large bowl with cold water and squeeze the juice of 2 lemons into it (reserve the lemon halves). Snap off several layers of leaves from each artichoke, pulling them downward to break them off at the base. Rub the cut parts often with the lemon halves as you work to prevent discoloration. Cut off the top of each artichoke and trim the broken parts of leaves around the stem with a sharp knife, again rubbing the cut surfaces with lemon. Halve the artichokes and remove the center chokes with a knife or grapefruit spoon; drop each prepared artichoke into the bowl of lemon water. Drain just before adding to the pan.

PESCADO CON AGRISTADA
Make avgolemono with 2 cups of boiling vegetable, fish, or chicken stock to create the ideal sauce for poached, grilled, or fried fish. The sauce can also be used with poached chicken.

WINTER VARIATION
Substitute 4 quartered celery hearts for the artichokes or use a bunch of leaf celery and peeled and sliced celery root. Cook as directed.

✦ Lamb Tagine ✦
with Dried Figs and Sesame Seeds

The combination of salty, sour, fragrant, and sweet tastes is the most obvious characteristic of Moroccan cuisine. In general, Moroccan dishes are not as fiery as those from Algeria or Tunisia. I first tasted this lamb and fig tagine in the restaurant Silia in Marrakech. Later I found a similar recipe in Hayat Dinia's book *La Cuisine Marocaine de Rabat*. The recipe that follows is my interpretation of this deeply flavored tagine. Serve with couscous or with toasted crusty pita bread. Makes 6 servings

$1/3$ cup olive oil or a combination of olive oil and unsalted butter

3 pounds lamb shoulder with some bone, cut into roughly 2-inch chunks

5 garlic cloves, coarsely chopped

1 teaspoon coarsely ground black pepper, plus more to taste

$1/2$ to 1 teaspoon Ras el Hanout (page 13)

Pinch of ground turmeric

Generous pinch of saffron threads

2 pounds dried figs, soaked in water for 3 hours

1 tablespoon honey

2 cinnamon sticks, 2 to 3 inches long

Sea salt

2 tablespoons red wine vinegar, or to taste

3 tablespoons toasted sesame seeds (see page 213)

Put the olive oil in a large sauté pan over low heat. Add the lamb and sauté until firm, about 10 minutes. Add the garlic and sauté a little longer without letting it color.

Add 1 teaspoon of the pepper, the ras el hanout, turmeric, and saffron and pour in about 2 quarts water. Bring to a boil, lower the heat, and simmer, covered, for about 1 hour, until the lamb is tender.

Meanwhile, put the figs, 2 tablespoons of their soaking liquid, the honey, and the cinnamon sticks in a separate pan. Bring to a boil and cook over high heat for about 10 minutes, until caramelized.

Check the lamb, which should be very tender. Season with salt and pepper to taste.

Remove the lamb from the pan with a slotted spoon, cover, and keep warm. Add the vinegar to the pan and cook over high heat to reduce the liquid to about $1^1/2$ cups. Add the lamb and figs, together with their juices, to the sauce and cook for another 2 minutes, just to warm through. Sprinkle with the toasted sesame seeds and serve.

Pork Tenderloin with Chile and Vinegar

This recipe comes from Molise—the narrow hilly strip of Italy between Abruzzo and Apulia. It was given to me by Princess Marina Colonna, who produces some of the best Italian extra virgin and citrus-scented olive oils in southern Italy. A local trattoria called La Carrese serves pampanella as its specialty. In many parts of southern Italy, a bowl of chopped dried peperoncini is placed on the table so everyone can add extra heat to all kinds of dishes. Marina told me that the region's hottest dishes were probably introduced by Albanians, who emigrated to Molise long ago. Serve pampanella with French fries or mashed potatoes. Makes 4 servings

3 or 4 dried peperoncini or chiles de árbol, snipped with scissors, to taste

4 or 5 garlic cloves, minced, to taste

$1^1/2$ pounds pork tenderloin, trimmed of all fat and cut into $2/3$-inch-thick medallions

2 to 3 tablespoons extra virgin olive oil

Coarse sea salt

2 to 3 tablespoons good-quality white wine vinegar

Mix the chopped chiles and garlic. Spread the mixture evenly on both sides of each pork medallion 3 or 4 hours before grilling or the night before. Cover and refrigerate.

Preheat the broiler.

Drizzle the pork with olive oil, sprinkle with salt, and broil close to the heat source for 5 or 6 minutes, until cooked, turning once. You can also cook the pork on a griddle. Splash with vinegar as you take the meat out of the oven, sprinkling with a little more peperoncini if you like. Serve immediately.

VARIATION
You can substitute skinless, boneless chicken breasts or turkey cutlets for the pork.

✦ Slow-Roasted Pork ✦
with Garlic, Rosemary, and Peperoncini

This roasted pork is inspired by the Tuscan arista alla Fiorentina. I've added chiles to the recipe, and I let the meat marinate rubbed in the garlicky paste at least overnight and preferably for twenty-four hours. The pork is roasted covered, and the meat bathes in its fragrant juices. The juicy meat is browned, uncovered, only during the last thirty minutes. This pork roast is ideal for parties, and you will enjoy the leftovers in sandwiches, or you can chop and add them to All-Purpose Greek Tomato Sauce (page 22) to create a memorable ragù sauce for pasta. Makes 8 to 10 servings

5 garlic cloves, finely chopped

1/4 cup olive oil

1 tablespoon chopped fresh rosemary leaves, plus 4 fresh rosemary sprigs

3 or 4 dried peperoncini or chiles de árbol, thinly sliced or snipped with scissors, to taste

1 teaspoon sea salt

One 4- to 5-pound boneless pork loin roast or top leg (fresh ham), trimmed of most fat

4 or 5 medium red onions, halved

In a small bowl, combine the garlic, olive oil, chopped rosemary, chiles and salt. Rub the garlic paste all over the pork, making several deep incisions and filling them with the paste. With kitchen twine, tie the rosemary sprigs along the sides of the pork, then place the pork in a deep pan or Dutch oven that will hold the meat snugly. Cover with aluminum foil and then the lid and refrigerate overnight or for up to 24 hours.

Preheat the oven to 400°F.

Remove the aluminum foil, replace the lid, and bake for 30 minutes. Reduce the oven temperature to 375°F, add the onion halves around the pork, and bake for about 1 hour more, basting twice with the pan juices. Uncover, baste again, and bake, uncovered, for about 30 minutes more, or until an instant-read thermometer inserted into the thickest part registers 155° to 165°F.

Remove the pork from the oven, cover, and let rest for 10 to 20 minutes to develop the flavors. Slice, and serve with the onions.

Grilled Skewered Sausage-Shaped Patties

All over the Middle East, ground meat kebab is a popular street food. It is served with pita bread and chopped vegetables, often complemented with hummus, tarator (garlic sauce), or tzatziki (yogurt, garlic, and cucumber sauce). These skewered sausagelike burgers are made with fatty lamb or mutton in the Arab countries and a combination of pork and beef in Greece, combined with finely chopped onion and a choice of spices—different in each part of the region. In the Turkish adana kebab the onion is mixed with tangy sumac, and the very flavorful Maraş pepper flakes add a kick to the ground lamb. The Lebanese kafta is aromatic with cinnamon and allspice. In her wonderful *Mediterranean Street Food,* my friend Anissa Helou describes eating camel *kefta* in Damascus. Compared to mutton, she says, "The meat did not taste very different— perhaps a little gamier, with a slightly drier texture."

In traditional adana kebab ground lamb is combined with fat, usually from the tail. Helou suggests using ground lamb shoulder, which is naturally fatty. I add fatty pork to my lean ground beef. Add allspice and cinnamon, if you like, for an aromatic kafta. Use flat metal or soaked bamboo skewers or sprigs of bay or rosemary for a more attractive presentation. Serve with warm pita bread and, if you like, with Ezme Salatasi (page 84).

Makes 4 to 6 servings

2^1/2 cups coarsely chopped onion

1 teaspoon sumac

Sea salt

2 to 4 teaspoons Aleppo or Maraş pepper, or a pinch of hot red pepper flakes, to taste

^{1}/2 cup fresh flat-leaf parsley leaves (optional)

2 pounds ground lamb shoulder, or 1 pound ground lean beef plus 1 pound ground fatty pork shoulder

^{1}/2 to 1 teaspoon ground cumin (optional)

Pinch of ground cinnamon (optional)

^{1}/2 teaspoon ground allspice (optional)

6 to 8 metal or bamboo skewers, preferably flat, soaked in water for a few minutes and drained on paper towels

Light a charcoal grill or preheat the broiler.

Put the onion, sumac, salt to taste, Aleppo pepper, and parsley if you're using it in a blender or food processor. Pulse to chop very fine.

Combine the ground meat with the onion mixture in a bowl. Add the spices if you like and knead thoroughly to combine. Take 1 teaspoon of the mixture, flatten it, and cook in a skillet, then taste and correct the seasoning. Cover and refrigerate the meat mixture for at least 1 hour and up to 4 hours.

Divide the meat mixture into 6 or 8 portions and shape each into an oblong patty. Take one patty on your hand and place the skewer on top, pressing the meat mixture to take the shape of a sausage around the skewer. Pinch the ends so that the mixture sticks to the skewers. Continue to shape the rest of the kebabs.

Grill very close to the heat source for 3 to 4 minutes, turn, and grill for another 3 to 4 minutes, depending on the size of the kebabs. You can also cook them on a griddle. Serve at once, with warm pita and salad.

Chicken Stuffed with Rice, Pine Nuts, and Preserved Lemon Slices

This is my interpretation of *dajaj mahshi,* a festive Palestinian dish I found in Aziz Shihab's book *A Taste of Palestine.* It is usually served to new brides and mothers.

Makes 5 to 6 servings

$^1/4$ cup plus 1 tablespoon olive oil

2 cups chopped onion

$^1/2$ cup pine nuts

1 cup long-grain rice

1 cup dry white wine

1 teaspoon Ras el Hanout (page 13)

One 3-inch cinnamon stick

1 teaspoon ground cumin seeds

3 to 5 teaspoons freshly ground black pepper

Sea salt

$^1/4$ cup finely diced Lemon Slices in Spicy Olive Oil (page 33), or 1 teaspoon grated lemon zest

1 chicken, about 3 pounds, preferably free-range

$^1/2$ cup Greek yogurt, preferably sheep's milk (see page 213)

3 to 5 teaspoons hot paprika, preferably Turkish, to taste

3 tablespoons chopped fresh cilantro

Warm the olive oil in a large sauté pan over medium-high heat. Add the onion and pine nuts and sauté until the onion is soft and the pine nuts turn golden, about 4 minutes. Add the rice and sauté for another 3 minutes, until the rice is translucent. Pour in half the wine and 2 cups water and cook, stirring, until all the liquid has evaporated, about 10 minutes. Add the ras el hanout, cinnamon, cumin, pepper, salt to taste, and lemon slices, stir, and adjust the seasonings.

Preheat the oven to 450°F.

Wash the chicken and pat dry with paper towels. Reserve the neck and giblets. Fill the cavity of the chicken loosely with rice (it will expand in cooking) and close the opening with skewers or tooth-picks. Keep the rest of the rice covered.

Mix the yogurt with the paprika and a little salt in a bowl. Baste the chicken with the yogurt mixture, then place the chicken in a pan or an ovenproof dish that will hold it, leaving about 1 inch of space all around. Pour the rest of the wine into the pan and add the neck and giblets. Cover with aluminum foil and bake for 1 hour. Uncover, reduce the heat to 400°F, and continue baking for 30 to 35 minutes, until the juices run clear when the thigh is pricked with a fork.

Remove the pan from the oven, transfer the chicken to another dish, and cover to keep warm. Add the remaining rice to the pan where the chicken has cooked and toss to mix with the drippings, adding $^1/3$ cup water. Place the chicken on top of the rice and transfer once more to the oven. Bake for another 20 minutes, until the rice is bubbly and the chicken has formed a nice crust. Sprinkle with cilantro and serve.

Broiled Chicken Wings
in Lemon-Honey-Chile Glaze

Simple, fast, and utterly irresistible, these chicken wings are briefly marinated with items from my pantry. If you don't have Lemon, Honey, and Pepper Jelly on hand, a mixture of lemon and honey with hot red pepper flakes will create an equally interesting spicy and aromatic glaze. I prefer to serve the wings as a main course, on a lunch or dinner buffet, together with one or two vegetable dishes and a salad. They can also be a warm appetizer, however, and are an ideal stand-up party food. Makes 6 to 8 servings

GLAZE

$1/4$ cup Lemon, Honey, and Pepper Jelly (page 26), or $1/4$ cup fresh lemon juice, slightly warmed, mixed with 1 tablespoon honey, preferably Greek, or to taste

3 garlic cloves, minced

1 tablespoon olive oil

1 tablespoon chopped fresh rosemary leaves

2 to 4 teaspoons Aleppo or Maraş pepper, or a pinch of hot red pepper flakes, to taste

1 teaspoon finely grated lemon zest

1 teaspoon ground cumin

1 tablespoon Dijon mustard

3 tablespoons white or rosé wine

Sea salt

3 pounds chicken wings, tips discarded, each wing separated into 2 pieces

Fleur de sel (optional)

In a bowl or other container large enough to hold all the wings, toss together the jelly, garlic, olive oil, rosemary, pepper, lemon zest, cumin, mustard, and wine. Sprinkle with about 1 teaspoon salt, stir, and add the chicken wings. Toss thoroughly, cover, and refrigerate for 2 to 3 hours or overnight, tossing once if possible.

Preheat the broiler. Line a baking sheet with aluminum foil.

Spread the wings in the pan in one layer. Broil 6 to 7 inches from the heat source, turning once, for 10 to 15 minutes on each side, until deep golden brown. Sprinkle with fleur de sel or some additional regular salt if you like and serve hot, warm, or even at room temperature.

✦ Chicken Tagine with Seasonal Vegetables ✦

Chicken or meat cooked with the season's best vegetables is a common dish throughout the Mediterranean. In its North African version the *tagine*, as the stew is called, is spiced with chiles or harissa and is cooked slowly in the traditional earthenware clay casserole with the conical cover—also called *tagine*—over a charcoal fire. I often serve the dish in the small individual tagine pots that I found in an ethnic store on the lower east side of Manhattan. Present the chicken tagine on its own or with couscous, but always with fresh crusty bread to dip in the delicious sauce. Makes 4 servings

1/4 cup olive oil

4 chicken thighs

1 1/2 cups chopped onion

3 to 6 fresh jalapeño chiles or pickled peperoncini (see page 215), chopped

1/2 cup dry white wine

4 medium artichokes, trimmed and halved (see Note, page 141)

1 cup fresh fava beans, green beans, or peas

2 cups thinly sliced carrot

1 1/2 cups finely chopped fresh flat-leaf parsley

1 teaspoon sea salt, or to taste

1/2 to 1 teaspoon Ras el Hanout (page 13)

2/3 cup chopped fresh dill

3 or 4 Lemon Slices in Spicy Olive Oil (page 33), rinsed and cut into 8 pieces (optional)

1 1/2 teaspoons cornstarch

3 tablespoons fresh lemon juice, or more to taste

Freshly ground black pepper

Warm the olive oil in a large sauté pan over medium-high heat. Add the chicken pieces and sauté until golden on all sides, about 10 minutes. Transfer to a plate with a slotted spoon and add the onion to the pan. Sauté until translucent, 2 to 3 minutes. Add the chiles and the chicken pieces to the pan. Pour in the wine and add the artichokes, fava beans, carrot, and parsley. Add the salt and ras el hanout, pour in 2 cups water, and bring to a boil. Lower the heat, cover, and simmer for 15 to 20 minutes, until the chicken and vegetables are cooked. Sprinkle with half the dill and add the lemons if you like. Dissolve the cornstarch in the lemon juice and pour it into the pan. Do not stir, but shake the pan to distribute. Let cook for 5 to 10 minutes, then taste and adjust the seasoning, adding freshly ground pepper to taste or more lemon juice if needed. Sprinkle with the rest of the dill just before serving.

✦ Slow-Cooked Chickpeas ✦
with Orange, Lemon, and Celery

There are countless variations of slow-cooked chickpeas all over the Mediterranean. Some are vegetarian, like this one, which is served traditionally with smoked or salted herring or sardines. Often chickpeas are cooked together with meat, as in the famous Spanish cocido. In the Cyclades, chickpeas are left to simmer overnight in the wood-burning oven. Kalomira Vrondamiti, the owner and cook of a tavern on the picturesque Vourkari marina in Kea, gave me this family recipe. I added extra chile, as well as mustard, something my mother adds to all legumes. Makes 6 to 8 servings

$2^1/2$ cups dried chickpeas

$1/4$ teaspoon baking soda

$1/3$ cup olive oil

2 cups coarsely chopped onion

1 or 2 jalapeño or other green or red fresh chiles, sliced

2 medium carrots, sliced

2 to 5 teaspoons Aleppo or Maraş pepper, or a pinch of hot red pepper flakes, to taste

$1^1/2$ cups chicken stock, or more as needed

One 4-inch piece fresh or dried orange peel

1 cup coarsely chopped celery, preferably leaf celery

2 tablespoons Dijon mustard

$1/4$ cup fresh lemon juice, or to taste

Sea salt and freshly ground black pepper

Extra virgin olive oil, preferably Greek, for drizzling

Soak the chickpeas overnight in plenty of water. Drain and rinse well under running water.

Preheat the oven to 400°F.

Combine the chickpeas with the baking soda in a medium bowl and toss well.

Heat the olive oil in a medium flameproof casserole over medium heat. Add the onion and sauté for 4 minutes, or until soft. Stir in the chiles, carrots, chickpeas, and Aleppo pepper, then add the stock, orange peel, and celery. Bring to a boil, remove from the heat, and cover the dish with a double layer of aluminum foil and then the lid.

Reduce the oven temperature to 250°F. Place the casserole in the oven and cook for 6 hours, or until the chickpeas are very tender. Add the mustard and lemon juice, taste, and adjust the seasonings, adding black pepper to taste. Drizzle with olive oil and serve hot, warm, or at room temperature.

Chicken Tagine with Seasonal Vegetables, page 152

Slow-Cooked Chickpeas with Orange,
Lemon, and Celery, page 153

Ayfer's Black-Eyed Pea, Ground Lamb, and Chard Stew

Ayfer Unsal is an outstanding cook and food writer from the Gaziantep—the part of southern Turkey that borders Syria. The one-pot meals of Gaziantep ingeniously combine seasonal vegetables, herbs, and greens with small amounts of meat to create delicious dishes that seem to be tailor-made by some modern nutritionist. Ayfer calls this stew *borani*—not to be confused with the vegetable and yogurt salads with the same name (page 88). Apparently the Turkish term *borani* is used for various stews and salads. This recipe is my adaptation of Ayfer Unsal's borani, from the book *Délices de Turquie,* which has been translated into many European languages, including Greek. Makes 4 servings

1 cup dried black-eyed peas

$^1/3$ cup olive oil

1 cup chopped onion

Sea salt and freshly ground black pepper (optional)

$^1/2$ pound lean ground lamb

1 to 2 tablespoons Turkish pepper paste (see Sources) or Harissa (page 19)

1 cup grated ripe fresh tomatoes (see page 212) or canned chopped tomatoes with their juice

1 to 3 teaspoons Aleppo or Maraş pepper or a pinch of hot red pepper flakes, to taste

1 cup dry white wine, vegetable stock, or water

Leaves from 1 bunch of chard, coarsely chopped

Place the peas in a medium saucepan, add cold water to cover by 2 inches, and bring to a boil. Cook for 5 minutes and drain.

Add fresh water to cover the peas and bring to a boil. Reduce the heat to low, cover, and simmer for about 15 minutes, or until the peas are just tender. Drain.

Warm the olive oil in a skillet or sauté pan over medium-high heat. Add the onion and sauté, sprinkling with salt to taste, for about 4 minutes, or until tender. Add the meat and sauté until firm and no longer pink, about 8 minutes. Add the pepper paste and toss for 30 seconds. Add the tomatoes, Aleppo pepper, peas, and wine. Bring to a boil, reduce the heat, and simmer for 10 minutes, or until the peas are very tender. Add the chard and toss to wilt. There should be only a little sauce in the pan; the dish must have the consistency of a moist pilaf. If it is too watery, increase the heat for a few minutes to reduce the sauce. Taste and add salt, along with pepper if you like. Serve in soup plates or bowls.

✦ Cranberry Bean and Potato Stew ✦ with Peppers and Spicy Sausage

We cook this dish in late summer with fresh shelled beans or throughout the year with frozen cranberry beans, which are called *handres* (beads) in Greek. Obviously, the fresh or frozen beans cook much faster than the dried ones and there is no need to soak or to discard the first cooking water. But the stew is equally good with dried cranberry or any other thin-skinned dried beans. Makes 4 to 6 servings

$2/3$ pound dried cranberry beans

$1/2$ cup olive oil

2 cups coarsely chopped onion

1 large green bell pepper, halved and sliced

1 large red bell pepper, halved and sliced

4 ounces spicy, preferably smoked, country sausage (Italian), chopped, or pancetta, cubed

2 or 3 pinches of Aleppo or Maraş pepper, or a pinch of hot red pepper flakes, to taste

2 cups canned diced tomatoes with their juice

3 cups vegetable or chicken stock

4 fresh thyme sprigs

Sea salt

2 medium potatoes, peeled and cut into 1-inch cubes

Fruity extra virgin olive oil, preferably Greek, for drizzling

$1/2$ cup chopped fresh flat-leaf parsley or cilantro

Soak the beans in plenty of water overnight.

Drain the beans, place in a pot, cover with cold water by 3 inches, and bring to a slow boil. Lower the heat, simmer for 30 minutes, and drain.

In the same pot, warm the olive oil over medium-high heat, add the onion and peppers, and sauté for about 6 minutes. Add the sausage and sauté for another 2 minutes. Add the Aleppo pepper and drained beans, turn a few times to coat with the oil, and pour in the tomatoes and stock. Bring to a boil, add the thyme and salt to taste, lower the heat, and simmer, partially covered, for about 40 minutes, until the beans are almost done, adding a little water as it evaporates. The beans should be quite juicy. Add the potatoes and cook for another 10 to 15 minutes, until tender.

Taste and adjust the seasoning. Serve in bowls, drizzled with fruity olive oil and sprinkled with parsley.

Thin Pasta with Uncooked Tomato Sauce

Although chiles provide a fair amount of heat, the dominant taste is the fresh, uncooked (*crude* in Italian) tomatoes. *Crudaiola* is the name given to the dish in Apulia, the heel of the Italian boot, but similar sauces are prepared in Sicily and all over the Italian South. Extremely versatile, the uncooked tomato sauce is ideal for pasta but can also be used as a topping for bruschetta or as a dressing for cooked beans or grilled meat or poultry. You must make it when tomatoes are at their best—red and meaty. Because I like it so much, I freeze several batches of fresh summer tomato pulp to make it even in winter (see page 212). Makes 3 to 4 servings

2 pounds ripe but firm summer tomatoes (see Note, page 96)

Coarse sea salt

2 or 3 garlic cloves, minced

$1/2$ cup extra virgin olive oil, plus oil for drizzling

3 tablespoons capers, preferably salt-packed, rinsed well, drained, and chopped

2 to 6 jalapeño or other green or red fresh chiles, finely chopped

$2/3$ cup chopped fresh flat-leaf parsley

$1/2$ cup torn fresh basil leaves

1 pound capellini or thin spaghetti

$1^{1}/2$ cups ricotta dura or hard mizithra cheese (see Sources), grated

To peel the tomatoes, dip into boiling water for 30 seconds, remove, rinse under cold water, and remove the skin. Cut out the stem, halve, and squeeze each half to get rid of most of the seeds, then chop.

Transfer the chopped tomatoes to a colander, sprinkle with a little salt, and let drain for 15 to 30 minutes. (Save the liquid for another use; it is very tasty.)

About 20 minutes before serving, mix the garlic with the olive oil, capers, chiles, and half the parsley and basil in a bowl. Add the tomatoes to the olive oil mixture, toss thoroughly, taste, and adjust the seasoning. The sauce should have a sharp taste.

Boil the pasta in salted water, following the package instructions. Drain and drizzle with olive oil, toss with the sauce, sprinkle with half the cheese and the remaining chopped herbs, and serve, passing the rest of the cheese at the table.

Pasta with Beans

Of all the different varieties of pasta, I have found that orecchiette ("little ears")—which are the traditional pasta of Apulia, in southern Italy—or the open shells are best suited for pasta e fagioli. Somehow a bean seems to end up resting inside the curve of each piece of pasta. In Apulia the dish is made with fresh homemade pasta. This recipe is my own adaptation of the dish I tasted at the Trattoria Cucina Casareccia in Lecce. Frying a handful of pasta adds another dimension to the dish. But even if you omit that step, you will love the spicy pasta e fagioli. If you can't get pancetta coated with red pepper flakes or *diavoletti*, the hot sausages of Calabria, use good-quality spicy chorizo. Makes 4 servings

2 cups fresh cranberry beans, or 1 cup dried cranberry beans soaked in water overnight

$1/3$ cup olive oil, plus oil for frying the pasta

1 cup chopped onion

1 teaspoon minced garlic

$3^1/2$ ounces chopped pancetta Calabrese (pancetta coated in hot red pepper flakes) or ordinary pancetta or chorizo, sliced

3 to 5 teaspoons Aleppo or Maraş pepper, or a pinch of hot red pepper flakes, to taste

$1/2$ cup dry white wine

$1^1/2$ cups grated ripe fresh tomatoes (see page 212) or good-quality canned chopped tomatoes with their juice

Sea salt

1 pound orecchiette or small pasta shells

3 tablespoons chopped fresh flat-leaf parsley (optional)

5 to 6 tablespoons grated Parmesan cheese (optional)

If you're using soaked dried beans, drain them, rinse with cold water, and bring to a boil. Lower the heat and simmer for 45 to 60 minutes, until the beans are almost soft but still firm. Drain.

Warm the olive oil in a heavy pot over medium-high heat. Add the onion and sauté for 2 to 3 minutes, until translucent. Add the garlic, pancetta, 2 teaspoons of the Aleppo pepper, and the beans. Sauté for another 2 minutes, until the water has evaporated. Pour in the wine. Cook over high heat for 30 seconds, then add the tomatoes and about 1 cup water. Bring to a boil, then lower the heat and simmer for 20 to 30 minutes, until the beans are very tender, adding water if needed. Season to taste with salt and more Aleppo pepper.

Cook the pasta until al dente and drain. If you like, halfway through cooking, take about a handful of orecchiette or shells out of the pot with a slotted spoon. Drain on a kitchen towel and fry in 1 inch hot olive oil until golden and crunchy. Drain on paper towels.

Mix the cooked pasta with the bean mixture. Cover and let stand for 5 minutes.

Add the fried pasta and toss. Taste and adjust the seasoning.

Serve very warm, sprinkled with parsley, Parmesan cheese, or both if you like.

Fettuccine with Chickpeas and Peperoncini

The unusual combination of pasta and chickpeas comes from Apulia, on the heel of the Italian boot. It is served drizzled with *diauliciu* ("the devil's condiment"), as chile olive oil is called in many parts of the Italian South. All the versions I tasted were made with fresh homemade pasta, part of which was fried, adding a wonderful crunch to the dish. You can achieve a similar effect with dried store-bought pasta (see Note).

Makes 4 servings

1 cup dried chickpeas, soaked in water overnight, or 3 cups cooked chickpeas (see page 211)

$1/2$ cup olive oil

1 pound homemade fettuccine or store-bought dried pasta, preferably linguine

4 garlic cloves, thinly sliced

3 to 5 dried peperoncini or 2 to 3 chiles de árbol, thinly sliced with scissors, to taste

Sea salt and freshly ground black pepper

1 cup vegetable or chicken stock (optional)

2 to 3 tablespoons fresh lemon juice

$1/2$ cup chopped fresh flat-leaf parsley

Peperoncini sott'Olio (page 36)

If you're using dried chickpeas, drain and cook in plenty of water over low heat for an hour, or until tender. Drain the chickpeas, but reserve 1 cup of the cooking liquid.

Warm the olive oil in a large heavy skillet over medium heat. Add about a quarter of the fresh pasta and fry until crisp, about 6 minutes. Remove with a slotted spoon and drain on paper towels. If you are using dried pasta, see the Note.

In the same olive oil, sauté the garlic and chiles over medium-high heat for less than a minute, without letting the garlic color. Add the cooked chickpeas, sprinkle with salt to taste, and sauté for 2 to 3 minutes. Pour in the reserved cooking liquid or the stock and cook for another 3 minutes. Stir in the lemon juice, taste, and add plenty of freshly ground black pepper and more lemon juice or salt if you like. You can prepare the dish a few hours in advance up to this point.

About 20 minutes before serving, cook the pasta until al dente, following the package instructions, drain it, and add it to the simmering chickpeas. Crumble the fried pasta, add to the skillet, toss, and adjust the seasoning. Sprinkle with chopped parsley and serve, drizzling each plate with some of the olive oil from the Peperoncini sott'Olio.

Note

If you are using store-bought dried pasta, boil a handful for 4 to 5 minutes, until it starts to soften. Drain well on paper towels and then fry it in olive oil until crisp.

✦ Penne all'Arrabbiata with Eggplant ✦

The "enraged" sauce—*arrabbiare* means "to get furious" or "red with anger"—refers to the fiery peperoncini that are the sauce's most prominent ingredient. This classic tomato and chile pasta is often served enriched with fried eggplant. Makes 4 servings

1 medium eggplant, about 1 pound, peeled in strips and cut into 1^1/2-inch cubes

Sea salt

^{1}/2 cup all-purpose flour

^{1}/2 cup olive oil, or more as needed

1 cup chopped onion

3 garlic cloves, sliced

2 to 4 dried peperoncini or other small chiles, cut in half lengthwise with scissors but left attached at the stem, or 2 to 4 teaspoons Aleppo or Maraş pepper, or a pinch of hot red pepper flakes, to taste

^{1}/2 cup dry white wine

2 cups grated ripe fresh tomatoes (see page 212) or good-quality canned diced plum tomatoes

Pinch of sugar

1 pound penne or bucatini

^{1}/2 cup grated pecorino Romano cheese

Shavings of Parmesan cheese (optional)

3 tablespoons chopped fresh flat-leaf parsley

Sprinkle the eggplant generously with salt, toss, and place in a colander. Let drain for at least 30 minutes. Squeeze with paper towels to extract as much liquid as possible, then dry the eggplant pieces with paper towels. Toss with the flour to coat well.

Warm the olive oil in a large skillet over medium-high heat, testing it with a piece of eggplant. If it sizzles vigorously, the oil is hot enough. Sauté the eggplant, tossing, until golden brown, about 4 minutes, adding a little more olive oil as needed. Remove with a slotted spoon and place in a colander over a bowl to collect the draining oil.

Using the remaining olive oil or the oil that has drained from the eggplant, sauté the onion in the skillet for 3 to 4 minutes, until translucent. Add the garlic and chiles and sauté for 1 minute more. Pour the wine into the skillet and cook over high heat for 30 seconds. Add the tomatoes and sugar, lower the heat, and simmer until most of the liquid has evaporated, 15 to 20 minutes.

Cook the pasta in plenty of salted water until al dente, following the instructions on the package. Drain, transfer to a warm bowl, pour the sauce over it, add the fried eggplant pieces and grated cheese, and toss. Taste to adjust the seasoning, adding more cheese if you like. Sprinkle with shavings of Parmesan if you wish, along with chopped parsley, and serve.

Baked Rice with Sweet and Hot Peppers, Scallions, and Feta

This easy and very forgiving rice casserole can be prepared in advance and enjoyed at room temperature, as a one-pot meal or as part of a buffet lunch or dinner. I have considered two different recipes: *riso forte*, a peppery rice pasticcio from Giuliano Bugialli's book *The Fine Art of Italian Cooking*, and a peasant Albanian rice dish. In both cases the rice cooks in milk, but the more refined Italian casserole is flavored with a combination of Gorgonzola, Parmigiano-Reggiano, and eggs, while the Albanian rice includes just feta cheese and yogurt, with plenty of scallions and dill, which give it a fresher taste. I choose to cook the latter more often, especially in the summer. Serve for lunch with just a tomato salad or as side dish, together with grilled fish or poultry.

Makes 4 to 6 servings

$^1/_3$ cup olive oil

$2^1/_2$ cups chopped scallion, including most of the green

2 green bell peppers, diced

3 or 4 jalapeño chiles, finely chopped

$1^1/_2$ cups medium-grain rice, such as Arborio

1 pound feta cheese, coarsely diced

1 cup Greek yogurt, preferably sheep's milk (see page 213)

1 cup chopped fresh dill

Freshly ground black pepper

About 1 quart whole milk, as needed

Preheat the oven to 400°F.

Heat the olive oil in a large skillet over medium-high heat. Add the scallion, bell peppers, and chiles and sauté until soft, about 6 minutes.

Add the rice and sauté for 2 minutes more. Remove from the heat and let cool slightly, then stir in the feta, yogurt, and dill. Add some freshly ground pepper and transfer to a $2^1/_2$-quart baking dish. Stir in $3^1/_2$ cups of the milk and bake for 20 minutes. Stir with a spatula and continue baking for 20 minutes, adding the rest of the milk as needed until the rice is cooked and has absorbed the milk. Let cool for 10 to 15 minutes and serve warm or at room temperature.

Pasta with Anchovies or Sardines, Fennel, Chile, and Pine Nuts

As its name suggests, this wonderful Sicilian pasta, my favorite, is originally made with salted sardines, or *sarde*—a Mediterranean staple. In some recipes fresh fried sardines complement the dish, served alongside the pasta. Cheap fish for the poor since antiquity, the sardines of the Mediterranean have now been transformed into a rare gourmet delicacy in the United States, imported from Italy, Spain, or France (see Sources). But they are not a household item, so I prefer to give you the anchovy version of the dish, which may sound more ordinary, but it is equally delicious. Get the best-quality, meatiest anchovies, preferably in olive oil, and use as many as you like, together with some of their oil. Fennel is the other crucial ingredient. The thick, intensely aromatic *Finocchio selvatico* (wild fennel) that the recipe asks for grows all over the Italian South—and, fortunately, on the Greek islands. But you can find it in the United States only occasionally, so I suggest a combination of fennel bulb, fennel fronds, and fennel seeds as an alternative with similar flavor. This sauce works best with bucatini (or perciatelli), the commercial hollow spaghetti. Makes 4 to 6 servings

$1/3$ cup sultanas (golden raisins)

Pinch of saffron threads (optional)

2 fennel bulbs, 1 sliced and 1 chopped

1 pound bucatini or perciatelli

$1/4$ cup olive oil

3 or 4 garlic cloves, chopped, to taste

$2/3$ cup chopped fresh wild fennel or cultivated fennel fronds plus $1/2$ to 1 teaspoon freshly ground fennel seeds

4 to 6 or more good-quality anchovy fillets or imported salted sardines, chopped, or more to taste (see Note)

2 to 4 dried peperoncini or chiles de árbol, thinly sliced or snipped with scissors, or 2 to 4 teaspoons Aleppo or Maraş pepper, or a pinch of hot red pepper flakes, to taste

4 to 5 tablespoons Anchovy and Peperoncino Olive Oil (page 31) or extra virgin olive oil, or more to taste

$1/4$ cup toasted pine nuts (see page 213)

Freshly ground black pepper and sea salt (optional)

In separate small bowls, soak the sultanas in about 1 cup warm water and the saffron threads, if using them, in 3 tablespoons warm water. Fill a large pot with water and bring to a rolling boil. Add the sliced fennel bulb and the bucatini and cook until the pasta is al dente, following the package instructions.

Meanwhile, warm the olive oil in a large heavy skillet over medium heat. Add the chopped fennel bulb and sauté for about 3 minutes. Add the garlic, wild fennel, fennel seeds, chopped anchovies, and peperoncini. Cook, stirring and mashing the anchovies with a wooden spoon, for 6 to 7 minutes, until the fennel is tender. Drain the sultanas and add to the skillet, together with the saffron and its liquid. Toss for 1 minute and remove from the heat.

Drain the pasta, reserving a little of the cooking liquid. Chop the boiled fennel and add it to the sauce along with $1/4$ cup of the cooking liquid and the drained pasta. Drizzle with the Anchovy and Peperoncino Olive Oil, add the pine nuts, and toss well. If too dry, add a bit more cooking liquid. Taste, add pepper and salt if you like, and serve at once.

Note
Look for anchovies imported from Spain or Italy and sold in jars, preserved in olive oil.

Pasta with Anchovies or Sardines,
Fennel, Chile, and Pine Nuts, page 166

Orzo "Risotto" with Fresh Favas,
Lemon, and Feta, page 170

Orzo "Risotto"
with Fresh Favas, Lemon, and Feta

Favas, planted in late fall, are the easiest crop to grow in our garden. They develop slowly during the winter, and in early spring they bloom, starting to fill with long velvety beans soon after. We usually eat the whole tender pods, chopping them to add to risotto or cooking them with artichokes, with plenty of lemon and wild fennel. As the spring progresses, the pods get bigger and are no longer tender, so we shell them, cooking just the green fava beans. They are so plentiful that even after offering baskets of them to friends and family I manage to keep bags of shelled favas in the freezer for the whole summer. From our two lemon trees we have fragrant fresh lemons all year, so this orzo is something that I very often whip up for lunch, when I am too busy with other things to plan a more elaborate meal. I wasn't expecting it, but this simple pasta has become the favorite dish of the people who attend our Kea Artisanal cooking classes. In early summer I make it with shredded zucchini and in the winter with shredded cabbage or spinach leaves (see the variations). Makes 4 servings

$1/2$ cup olive oil

4 or 5 garlic cloves, thinly sliced

4 cups shelled and peeled fresh or frozen favas

1 cup chopped fresh fava pods or green beans

Sea salt and freshly ground black pepper

1 pound orzo

2 to 4 teaspoons Aleppo or Maraş pepper, or a pinch of hot red pepper flakes, to taste

$1/2$ cup dry white wine

7 to 8 cups chicken or vegetable stock, very hot

$1/4$ cup fresh lemon juice

1 cup feta cheese, mashed with a fork, plus cheese for serving

3 tablespoons grated lemon zest

2 tablespoons chopped fresh dill or fennel fronds for serving (optional)

Heat the olive oil in a sauté pan over medium heat. Add the garlic, favas, and fava pods and sauté for 5 minutes. Add some salt, the pasta, and the Aleppo pepper and sauté for another 5 minutes. Add the wine, stir for 30 seconds, and pour in 3 cups of the very hot broth. Cook, stirring often and adding broth as the pasta absorbs the liquid, until the orzo is cooked al dente, about 20 minutes.

Remove from the heat and fold in the lemon juice, 1 cup feta, the zest, and freshly ground pepper to taste. Taste and correct the seasoning. Sprinkle with some more feta and the dill if you like, and serve immediately, with more feta in a bowl.

VARIATIONS

Substitute 4 cups grated tender zucchini or squash for the favas or make the dish with a combination of favas and sliced artichokes (see Note, page 141, for artichoke preparation) or shelled fresh peas. In the winter, make it with 4 to 5 cups of shredded cabbage or with spinach (about $1^1/2$ pounds leaves and stems).

Spicy Bulgur and Buckwheat Pilaf ⋅ with Peppers, Feta, Nuts, and Cilantro

I like to make this pilaf for our summer meals because I can serve it at room temperature since it is cooked with olive oil. Any leftovers can be transformed into a salad the next day, with tomatoes, grilled vegetables, and herbs. Hot and spicy bulgur or mixed-grain pilafs accompany kebabs—skewered grilled meat—in the Middle East. Pilafs are often eaten mixed with thick yogurt. I like the yogurt better with rice, though, and prefer to add feta to the bulgur pilaf. Its salty and tart flavor perfectly complements the spicy but sweet grains and nuts. If your local supermarket doesn't carry coarse bulgur, check ethnic markets and health food stores. Makes 4 servings

$1/4$ cup olive oil

1 medium onion, chopped

2 large red bell peppers, diced

2 to 5 teaspoons Aleppo or Maraş pepper, or a pinch of hot red pepper flakes, to taste

2 garlic cloves, minced

1 cup coarse bulgur

$1/2$ cup buckwheat

$1/2$ cup dry white wine

2 to $2^{1}/2$ cups vegetable or chicken stock, as needed

Sea salt

$1/2$ cup blanched sliced almonds, toasted (see page 213)

$1^{1}/2$ cups crumbled feta cheese

$1/4$ cup Dukkah (page 15), or $1/4$ cup pine nuts, toasted (see page 213)

$1/4$ cup chopped fresh cilantro

Warm the olive oil in a large saucepan over medium-high heat. Add the onion and sauté for 3 to 5 minutes, until translucent. Add the diced peppers and sauté for another 4 minutes, until wilted. Add the Aleppo pepper and garlic and stir a few seconds.

Rinse the bulgur and buckwheat under cold running water, until the water runs clear. Drain and add to the pepper mixture. Sauté for about 8 minutes, stirring constantly, then add the wine. Let boil for a few seconds, then pour in 2 cups of the stock and stir. Season with a little salt (the feta is usually quite salty). Boil vigorously for 2 minutes, then lower the heat and simmer for 5 minutes or more, until the bulgur and buckwheat are tender but not mushy. If the mixture seems too dry, add a little more stock.

Remove from the heat, stir in the almonds, cover the pan with a kitchen towel and the lid, and let stand for 5 to 10 minutes. Remove the lid and towel, add half the feta, and fluff with a fork, adding half the dukkah. Taste and adjust the seasoning, before spooning onto plates or into bowls. Sprinkle each plate with chopped cilantro, some more feta, and the rest of the dukkah. Serve hot, warm, or at room temperature.

◆ North African Soup ◆
with Capers, Harissa, and Cilantro

Coriander, caraway, fiery harissa, garlic, and fresh lemon juice give this vegetarian soup a typically North African flavor and aroma. The capers are an unusual addition. Makes 6 servings

1/4 cup olive oil

1 tablespoon minced garlic

1 1/2 teaspoons ground coriander seeds

1 tablespoon ground caraway seeds

1 teaspoon Harissa (page 19)

1 teaspoon Aleppo or Maraş pepper, or a
   pinch of hot red pepper flakes, to taste

1 tablespoon tomato paste

1/4 cup fine semolina

1/3 cup coarse bulgur or Trahana (page 42)

3 to 4 tablespoons fresh lemon juice

1/2 cup capers, preferably salt-packed, rinsed
   well and drained

2 Lemon Slices in Spicy Olive Oil (page 33),
   julienned (optional)

Sea salt

1/4 cup chopped fresh cilantro

Mix the olive oil with the garlic, coriander, caraway, harissa, and Aleppo pepper in a saucepan over medium heat. Stir to warm, without letting the spices burn. Add the tomato paste and stir for 30 seconds.

Pour in 4 cups water and bring to a boil. Add the semolina and bulgur, stirring constantly. Simmer for 10 to 15 minutes, then add the lemon juice, capers, and preserved lemon if you're using it. Cook until the grains are tender, about 6 minutes longer, adding more water if it is too thick. Taste and season with salt if needed. Serve warm, sprinkled with cilantro.

BREADS
and
DESSERTS

UNFORTUNATELY, THE QUALITY OF BREAD IS DECLINING SHARPLY throughout the Mediterranean region. Only a few bakers still get up early to make the dough the traditional way and let it rise for five to six hours. Even breads baked in traditional-looking wood-burning ovens are made using premixed flours and fast-acting yeasts that make the dough rise in a mere hour. The results are far from satisfying—flavorless, insubstantial loaves that can be enjoyed only when still warm. Many Turkish restaurants, especially the ones serving kebabs, following the old tradition, continue to bake individual flattish loaves in their kitchen and bring them to the table piping hot, directly from the oven. Food—mezedes and main courses—is always complemented with bread or pita in the Mediterranean, considered an essential part of any meal. I regularly bake the whole wheat bread we consume, using a sourdough starter that I began a long time ago, fermenting honey with barley flour. This method works best if you bake at least once a week, each time keeping a piece of dough for the next bread. For the occasional baker, the starter I propose works very well too.

Besides bread, paximadia (barley rusks), other savory biscotti, or simply twice-baked leftover bread slices are served with drinks, salads, soups, and spreads. The traditional cookies and biscotti in this chapter are a real treat with coffee, tea, and sweet wine. Twice-baked slices of savory bread or cake keep well for a long time and are great snacks and indispensable pantry items.

I chose to include only a few desserts and to forgo the obvious syrup-drenched baklava and its countless variations. The sweets I propose, like the Feta and Mizithra (Ricotta) Cheesecake (page 193), are the ones I make for my friends and family time and again. I have also included a simple fruity strawberry drink because I find it the perfect conclusion to any Mediterranean meal.

✦ Basic Bread with Spices ✦

For my everyday bread I use a combination of flours—fine semolina, whole wheat, and some barley flour, together with the standard all-purpose white flour. I grind together a few spices—coriander seeds, mahlep, caraway or cumin, mastic (see "Herbs, Flavorings, and Spices," page 4)—to make my Bread Spice Mixture. The inspiration comes from the traditional festive Greek breads, which are very aromatic with all sorts of spices and even herbs. Baked covered, in a preheated clay or heavy cast-iron casserole, the bread gets a wonderful thick crust. I use the same dough to make flat breads that I top not only with all sorts of seasonal vegetables and herbs but also with fresh or marinated sardines and anchovies. I serve these focaccia-like breads on their own, with a glass of wine, or together with the salads and spreads that I lay on the table before serving the main course. Makes 1 large or 2 medium loaves

1$^1/2$ cups fine semolina flour

2$^1/2$ cups unbleached all-purpose flour

2$^1/2$ cups whole wheat flour, or 1$^1/2$ cups whole wheat plus 1 cup barley flour

1 teaspoon active dry yeast (or 1$^1/2$ teaspoons if without starter)

2 teaspoons sea salt

1 tablespoon Bread Spice Mixture (page 11)

$^1/2$ teaspoon freshly ground white pepper

2 cups Starter (optional; recipe follows)

3 cups or more spring water

Place the flours, yeast, salt, and spices in a large bowl and mix well with a spatula. Make a well in the center and add the starter if you're using it and 3 cups water. Use the spatula to incorporate the liquids without overmixing. With a handheld mixer fitted with a dough hook, work the mixture for 1 to 2 minutes. Let stand for 15 minutes. Work again with the handheld mixer for 3 to 4 minutes or more, stopping occasionally to turn the dough over with a large spatula. The dough should still be wet and sticky but should start to pull away from the sides of the bowl. If too dry, add a little water; if too wet, add a few tablespoons all-purpose flour.

Flour the working surface and turn out the dough. Dust your hands and the dough with flour and, with the help of a large spatula, fold, push, turn, and fold the dough again for 2 to 3 minutes.

Lightly oil a large transparent or semitransparent bowl, as well as a piece of plastic wrap. With the help of the spatula, shape the dough into a ball and transfer to the oiled bowl. Trace a line on the outside of the bowl to monitor the dough's expansion. Cover with the oiled plastic and let rise until double its original volume: 4 to 5 hours or more. (When the dough has expanded to about $1^1/2$ times its original size, you may transfer the bowl with the dough to the refrigerator and leave it overnight or for up to 24 hours. It will continue to rise slowly. Before proceeding further, bring to room temperature. Let stand for 2 to 3 hours.)

Turn the dough out onto a lightly floured surface and shape into a loaf, an 8 X 11-inch oval or an 8-inch round. Place in the center of a long sheet of parchment paper, cover with the oiled plastic wrap, and let rise for another hour—it won't rise much. (At this point, you can cut off pieces of dough, flatten them slightly, sprinkle with flour, wrap in parchment paper, and freeze in resealable plastic bags. You can defrost and bake later, within 3 months.)

Thirty minutes before baking, place a cast-iron or clay casserole with lid in the oven and preheat to 450°F.

Remove the hot casserole from the oven, open the lid, and carefully lift the parchment paper to transfer the bread into the casserole. Cut off and discard the overhanging paper. With scissors, make one or more diagonal cuts in the surface of the loaf. Cover the casserole and return to the oven. Bake for 25 minutes. Lower the temperature to 400°F, uncover the casserole, and continue baking for 25 to 30 minutes. Wearing oven mitts and using a spatula, remove the bread from the casserole and place directly on the oven rack. Bake for 10 minutes more, or until the bread sounds hollow when you tap it on the bottom. Let cool completely on a rack before slicing.

Starter

The slightly sour starter will add richness to your bread. You can keep the leftover starter in the refrigerator, feeding it with additional flour and water every now and then, to have it on hand whenever you feel like baking a Mediterranean-style bread.

Makes 2^1/3 cups, about 1 pound

^{1}/2 teaspoon active dry yeast

^{1}/3 cup warm water

3^1/2 cups all-purpose flour

One or two days before baking make the starter: Mix the yeast with the warm water in a 4-quart bowl. Stir well and gradually add 3^1/2 cups flour and 1^1/2 cups water. Mix to form a smooth, thick batter. Cover and let stand at room temperature for 24 to 48 hours. The mixture will triple in size and become bubbly.

Use as much starter as needed for the bread recipe and replenish the remaining starter for future use by adding 1 or 2 cups flour and about ^{2}/3 cup water. Stir and keep in a sealed container in the refrigerator. It will separate.

Bring to room temperature the night before baking, add 1 more cup flour and about ^{1}/2 cup water. Stir and let rise overnight.

BREAD WITH GREENS

Use 1 cup water and 2^1/2 cups mixed greens—chard, mustard greens, arugula, etc.—blanched and reduced to a pulp in a blender.

PUMPKIN AND ORANGE BREAD

Use 2 cups pureed baked pumpkin, 1 cup fresh orange juice, and about ^{1}/2 cup water. Add the grated zest of a large orange, preferably organic, to the spice mixture.

⋆ Flat Breads with Various Toppings ⋆

Halve the basic dough (page 177) to make two flat breads with different toppings.

Anchovy (or Sardine) and Onion Ring Flat Bread

Line a baking sheet with parchment paper and spread one piece of dough on it, pushing and stretching with wet fingers to cover the pan. Let the dough rest for 10 to 15 minutes.

Meanwhile, line the oven rack with unglazed tiles or a baking stone or place one empty baking sheet in the oven. Preheat the oven to 500°F.

Slice a medium onion into $1/4$-inch-thick rings. Arrange 20 to 25 marinated anchovy fillets (such as Spanish *boquerones*) or Italian salted sardine fillets, briefly rinsed and dried, on the dough. Add the onion rings, pressing lightly so they stick to the dough, and sprinkle with Aleppo or Maraş pepper or hot or smoked paprika.

Slide the parchment paper with the dough onto the heated stone or pan, sprinkle the inside of the oven with water from a plant mister, and bake for 3 minutes. Sprinkle once more, reduce the oven temperature to 375°F, and bake for 15 to 20 minutes or more, until the flat bread is well browned. Let cool on a rack for at least 15 minutes before cutting to serve.

Rosemary and Jalapeño Flat Bread

Line a baking sheet with parchment paper and spread one piece of dough on it as for the preceding flat bread. Let the dough rest for 10 to 15 minutes and then spread it with about 2 tablespoons fresh rosemary leaves and 2 or 3 jalapeños or pickled green or red chiles, thinly sliced. Sprinkle with coarse salt, plain or aromatic, and bake as in the preceding recipe.

Southern Italian Corn Bread with Cheese and Peperoncini

This yellow pizza, as its name implies, is a wonderful savory cake that is traditionally added to vegetable and greens soups in the Italian South. Unlike in American corn breads, here the cornmeal cooks in the milk until almost as thick as polenta, and then it is mixed with cheese, eggs, and hot peppers. This hearty corn bread is delicious on its own, but I also like to serve it with Sweet-and-Sour Eggplants with Nuts, Sultanas, Basil, and Peperoncino (page 49), with Borani (page 88), with plain grilled peppers or other vegetables and olives, or with any vegetable stew or salad. The combination can be a full meal or an appetizer, depending on the portion size. Dice any leftover bread, dry it in a low oven, and keep in an airtight bag to add to vegetable or bean soups.

Makes 6 to 8 servings

1 quart whole milk

7 ounces coarse stone-ground yellow cornmeal or polenta meal

$1/2$ to 1 teaspoon sea salt

$1/2$ cup olive oil, plus oil for drizzling

1 pound mixed grated cheeses—$1/2$ pound pecorino Romano or hard mizithra, $1/4$ pound Cheddar, and $1/4$ pound Greek manouri, ricotta salata, or mozzarella, or any combination of spicy and sweet cheeses you like

3 or 4 dried peperoncini or chiles de árbol, thinly sliced or snipped with scissors

5 large eggs, separated

Pour the milk into a heavy saucepan over medium heat, sprinkle the cornmeal over the milk, add salt and cook, stirring, for 15 minutes, until thickened.

Preheat the oven to 375°F.

Add $1/2$ cup olive oil to the cornmeal mixture and cook, stirring, for another 5 minutes. Remove from the heat and add the cheeses, chiles, and egg yolks, one at a time, stirring to incorporate fully.

Beat the egg whites in a large bowl until they form soft peaks. Carefully fold in the cornmeal mixture with a spatula.

Line a deep 12-inch round pan with parchment paper and pour in the cornmeal batter. Drizzle with olive oil and bake for about 30 minutes, until deep golden and firm. Let cool for 10 minutes and cut pieces to serve warm or at room temperature.

Flat Breads with Various Toppings, page 180

Chickpea Breads, page 184

✦ Chickpea Breads ✦

The recipe for this delicious, chewy bread was given to me by Mark Furstenberg, who made real French and Mediterranean breads available in Washington, D.C., when he started Marvelous Market and later BreadLine. I have adapted this recipe for the home baker. The starter, although not absolutely necessary, gives the bread better taste and texture.

Chickpea Bread is an ideal accompaniment to stews and tagines and makes wonderful sandwiches. It is not hot or spicy because it is supposed to be eaten with spicy foods. Nevertheless, if you want to serve it with a sweet cheese, such as ricotta, or with grilled vegetables, you can increase the amount of cayenne and cumin. Makes 4 breads

1 teaspoon active dry yeast ($1^1/2$ teaspoons without starter)

$1/4$ cup warm water

$1^1/2$ cups Starter (optional, page 179)

2 cups unbleached all-purpose flour, plus flour for the work surface

$1^1/2$ cups bread flour

$1/2$ cup barley flour

$1^1/2$ teaspoons sea salt

1 teaspoon ground cumin

$1/2$ teaspoon cayenne, or more to taste

$1/2$ cup plus 1 tablespoon mashed cooked (see page 211) or drained canned chickpeas

2 tablespoons whole milk (optional)

1 tablespoon caraway or sesame seeds (optional)

Mix the yeast with the warm water in a bowl. Mix with the starter if you're using it and stir vigorously.

Put the flours, salt, and spices in a food processor fitted with the dough hook and pulse to mix. With the motor running on low, add the yeast mixture, $1^1/2$ cups water, and the chickpeas. Work the dough for 3 minutes, adding a little more water if needed to form a soft, slightly sticky dough.

Lightly flour a work surface, transfer the dough to it, and sprinkle it with flour. Knead the dough briefly with your hands. Form into a ball, oil a large bowl, and place the dough in it, turning to oil all over. Let stand for about $1^1/2$ hours, until doubled in size.

Turn the dough onto the floured work surface, divide into 4 pieces, and shape each into a ball. Cover with oiled plastic wrap and let stand for 30 minutes. If you like, brush the dough balls with milk and sprinkle with caraway or sesame seeds. Or you can press the dough with a plate or with wet fingers to make flat breads.

Let the dough rest for another 10 to 15 minutes. Meanwhile, line the oven rack with unglazed tiles or a baking stone and preheat the oven to 500°F.

Place the breads on the stone and, with a razor blade or scissors, slash the tops once or twice. Bake for 25 minutes or more, until well browned.

⋆ Cretan Barley Rusks ⋆

This is a crunchier version of paximadia. Most traditional barley rusks, like the ones needed for the Paximadi Salad (page 95), become very hard when dried in the oven. These are made with a combination of barley and wheat flour and are crispy and light. For a first course or light lunch, top them with chopped fresh tomato, onions, and a little fresh chile. Then sprinkle with dried oregano, drizzle with extra virgin olive oil, and serve with feta cheese. Cretan Barley Rusks are the ideal accompaniment to most cheeses and all kinds of spreads, including the Eggplant, Pepper, and Parsley Spread (page 52) or the Olive, Almond, and Herb Spread (page 28). Makes sixteen $4^1/2$-inch biscuits

2 tablespoons honey

1 cup warm water, or more, as needed

2 tablespoons active dry yeast

1 tablespoon coarse sea salt

1 tablespoon aniseeds or star anise

2 to $2^1/2$ cups unbleached all-purpose flour

2 cups barley flour

$^1/2$ cup olive oil

$^1/2$ cup sweet red wine, such as Greek Mavrodaphne or port

$^1/2$ cup dry red wine

Olive oil for brushing the dough and baking sheets

Dissolve the honey in $^1/3$ cup of the warm water in a small bowl. Add the yeast, stir, and leave to proof for 10 minutes.

In a mortar, pound the salt with the aniseeds until you get a coarse powder. Sift the flours into a large bowl and stir in the aniseed-salt powder. Make a well in the center and pour in the olive oil, wines, yeast mixture, and another $^1/2$ cup warm water. Draw the flour toward the center, mixing it with the liquids to form a rather sticky dough. Knead patiently, adding a little more warm water or flour to make a smooth dough. (Alternatively, make this dough in a food processor or an electric mixer fitted with the dough hook. Add all the ingredients and process for 3 minutes at low speed. Scrape the bowl with a spatula, let rest for 5 to 10 minutes, then process for another 3 to 5 minutes.)

Turn the dough out onto a lightly floured board and continue kneading, folding, pushing, turning, and folding for another 3 minutes. You should end up with a soft, very slightly sticky dough. Form a ball, brush it all over with a few drops of olive oil, place in a 3-quart bowl, cover with plastic wrap, and let rise for about $1^1/2$ hours, until doubled in size.

Cut the dough in half and divide each piece into quarters. Form each piece into a 1-inch-thick cord, then shape each cord into a coil, a circle with overlapping ends. Place the circles on baking sheets lined with parchment paper, $1^1/2$ inches apart. Cover with plastic wrap and let rise for 1 more hour.

Preheat the oven to 400°F.

Put the bread circles in the oven and immediately reduce the temperature to 375°F. Bake for 30 to 40 minutes, until the bread circles are golden on top and sound hollow when tapped.

Let them cool for 10 minutes. Turn the oven down to its lowest setting (175°F). Using a very good bread knife, slice the circles in half horizontally. Place the halves on a cookie sheet and return to the oven for about $1^1/2$ to 2 hours, until they are completely dry. Let cool on a rack and store in tins in a dry place. They will keep for up to 6 months.

VARIATION
You can shape the dough into 4 baguettes. After baking, let cool for a few minutes, then slice into $1/2$-inch pieces. Dry as directed to make paximadakia (small paximadia).

◆ Peppery Olive Oil and Ouzo Biscotti ◆

These savory biscotti are a cross between the traditional crunchy Greek ouzo bread rings and the Italian taralli. Instead of shaping the dough into rings, I prefer to bake it first as a long baguette, then slice it and dry the pieces in a low oven, as we do for the sweet biscotti. Serve by themselves as a snack or to accompany cheese, salads, or mezedes such as the Eggplant, Pepper, and Parsley Spread (page 52), Feta and Pepper Spread (page 55), or Borani (page 88). Makes about 8 dozen biscuits

2 tablespoons honey, preferably thyme scented

1 cup warm water, or more as needed

$1^1/2$ tablespoons active dry yeast

$3^1/2$ to 4 cups unbleached all-purpose flour, or 1 cup whole wheat plus $2^1/2$ to 3 cups all-purpose flour

2 teaspoons coarsely ground black pepper, 2 to 3 teaspoons Aleppo or Maraş pepper, or a pinch of hot red pepper flakes, to taste

1 tablespoon ground aniseeds

$1^1/2$ teaspoons sea salt

$1/3$ cup ouzo, Pernod, or any other anise-flavored liqueur

$1/2$ cup olive oil, plus oil for brushing the dough

2 to 3 tablespoons nigella seeds (optional; see Sources)

Dissolve the honey in $1/3$ cup of the warm water in a small bowl. Stir in the yeast and leave to proof for 10 minutes.

Sift $3^1/2$ cups of the flour into a large bowl. Stir in the pepper, aniseeds, and salt. Make a well in the center and pour in the yeast mixture, ouzo, olive oil, and another $1/2$ cup warm water. Draw the flour toward the center, mixing it with the liquids to form a dough. Knead well for about 15 minutes, until you have a soft, smooth dough. Add a little more flour or water if needed. (Alternatively, make this dough in a food processor or an electric mixer fitted with the dough hook. Add all ingredients and process the mixture for 3 to 4 minutes.)

Turn the dough out onto a lightly floured board, knead for about 3 minutes, and shape it into a ball. Brush with oil and cover with plastic wrap, and let rise for about 2 hours, until doubled in size.

Turn the dough out onto a lightly floured board, punch it a few times, and divide into quarters. Shape each piece into a 1-inch-thick, 15-inch-long baguette. If you like, sprinkle with nigella. Place on a baking sheet lined with parchment paper, cover again with plastic wrap, and let rise for about 1 hour, until almost doubled in size.

Preheat the oven to 375°F.

Bake the loaves for 25 to 30 minutes, until they are golden brown and sound hollow when tapped. Cool on a rack for 15 to 20 minutes.

Turn the oven down to its lowert setting (175°F). Using a good bread knife, cut the baguettes into $1/2$-inch slices. Place the slices on a cookie sheet and return to the oven to dry completely, about 3 hours. Cool on a rack and store in airtight tins. If you don't devour them instantly, they will keep for up to 4 months.

PEPPERY MASTIC BISCOTTI
Substitute a flavorless spirit such as vodka for the ouzo and substitute mastic for the aniseed. Mix the mastic with the salt and pound in a stone or porcelain mortar to grind.

✦ Savory Cheese, Almond, and Chile Cookies ✦

Taking the principle from the sugar-coated Roasted Almond Cookies called *kourambiedes* (page 204), I came up with a savory version. These cookies have a similar crunchy texture and are as addictive as the sweet kourambiedes.

Makes about 30 cookies

2 cups all-purpose flour

$1^1/2$ teaspoons baking powder

1 cup coarsely ground toasted almonds (see page 213)

1 cup grated Parmesan cheese, preferably Parmigiano-Reggiano

$1/2$ to 1 teaspoon sea salt, to taste

1 teaspoon Aleppo or Maraş pepper or hot Hungarian paprika

$1/2$ to 1 teaspoon smoked paprika (pimentón)

$1/3$ cup lard or softened unsalted butter

$1/2$ cup olive oil

1 large egg, lightly beaten

1 tablespoon ouzo or vodka, or more as needed

Stir the flour, baking powder, almonds, cheese, salt, pepper, and smoked paprika together with a spatula in a bowl.

In another bowl, beat the lard or butter with the olive oil, egg, and 1 tablespoon ouzo.

Preheat the oven to 350°F.

Make a well in the center of the flour mixture and pour in the liquids. Work fast with a spatula or your hands to make an oily dough that barely holds together. If too dry, add a bit more ouzo or vodka. Don't overwork the dough. Let rest for 20 to 30 minutes.

Line 2 baking sheets with parchment paper. Halve the dough and flatten the first piece on a work surface to make a rectangle about $1/3$ inch thick. With a knife, cut the dough into roughly 1-inch strips and then each strip into $2^1/2$- to 3-inch-long finger-shaped biscuits. With a spatula, carefully transfer the biscuits to the baking sheets, leaving at least $1/2$ inch space between them. Repeat with the second piece of dough.

Bake the 2 baking sheets together for 15 to 20 minutes, until the biscuits start to brown, switching the position of the sheets halfway through the baking. Carefully transfer to a rack to cool. Keep in an airtight box for up to 2 weeks.

✦ Feta and Mizithra (Ricotta) Cheesecake ✦

I got the idea for this salty-sweet cheesecake from descriptions of ancient desserts, which freely combined sweet, savory, and spicy flavors. Apicius—who wrote the first surviving cookbook, in Roman times—lists a dessert made with fresh cheese and dried fruits. In Greece and Italy, many traditional sweets, especially the ones made for Easter, are prepared with fresh and lightly salted cheeses like ricotta and mizithra. In their older forms, these cheeses were made saltier so they would stay fresh without refrigeration in the warm climate. My feta and mizithra cheesecake is inspired by those old sweets and has a complex and very satisfying taste. Prepare at least one day in advance. Baked cheesecakes keep for 5 or 6 days in the refrigerator.

Makes 2 cheesecakes, serving 12 to 15

Sunflower oil for the pans

10 ounces soft feta cheese, crumbled

$1^2/3$ to 2 cups sugar, to taste

$1^1/3$ pounds mizithra or ricotta cheese, preferably sheep's milk

3 tablespoons cornstarch

3 tablespoons cream or whole milk

6 large eggs

Grated zest of 2 lemons or 1 lemon plus 1 orange or tangerine, preferably organic

Half of a 16-ounce package kataifi (shredded phyllo pastry)

4 tablespoons unsalted butter, melted, or sunflower oil

$1/2$ cup slivered almonds

2 cups kumquat, blood orange, or bitter orange preserves or marmalade

Oil two 9 X 5 X 3-inch loaf pans. Preheat the oven to 325°F.

In a food processor, blend the feta, $1^2/3$ cups sugar, and the mizithra (taste and add more sugar if you like). Dissolve the cornstarch in the cream and add to the cheese mixture. Add the eggs, one at a time, and the zest and process to make a smooth, creamy mixture.

Pour into the oiled pans and place both in a larger deep baking pan. Put in the bottom third of the oven and pour in enough hot water to reach halfway up the sides of the loaf pans. Bake for about 1 hour, until the cheesecakes set and their tops are puffed and deep golden. Remove from the oven and cool on a rack. Do not turn the oven off. As they cool, the cheesecakes will shrink and any cracks will disappear. When cold, cover the pans with foil and refrigerate overnight or for up to 5 days.

Line a baking sheet with parchment paper, tracing the size of the plate where you plan to serve the cheesecake. In a bowl, sprinkle the kataifi with melted butter and work with your fingers to oil all the threads. Transfer to the parchment paper and fill the tracing you made. Sprinkle with the almonds and bake for about 10 minutes on the middle rack, until light golden. Let cool and transfer to the serving platter. You can prepare the crust 1 to 5 days in advance, cover with foil or plastic, and let stand at room temperature.

To serve the cheesecake, run the blade of a knife around the sides of the pans and invert over the kataifi. Top with preserves or marmalade. As you cut servings, make sure you include pieces of the crunchy kataifi crust.

✦ Spicy Mastic Ice Cream ✦

Mastic (often confused with the flavorless gum arabic, which it resembles) is the fragrant resin from a member of the pistachio family that grows only on the Greek island of Chios. Used from antiquity all over the Middle East as a chewing gum and to flavor sweets, mastic is also an excellent flavoring for breads and cookies.

Salep (or sahlep), the powdered root of a species of wild orchid, was traditionally used to thicken ice cream, but it is difficult to find it in the United States, so use arrowroot or cornstarch instead. I add dried chile to this classic Greek ice cream, giving it an unexpected kick. Serve by itself or with fruit salads, fruit tarts, or cakes.

Makes 1 quart

6 large egg yolks

1 cup sugar

2 cups whole milk

1 dried chile de árbol, cut in half lengthwise with scissors

2 teaspoons arrowroot or cornstarch, dissolved in 3 tablespoons of the milk

1 teaspoon mastic, powdered in a mortar with a little granulated sugar (see Note)

1 cup Greek yogurt (preferably sheep's milk (see page 213), or cream

Beat the egg yolks with the sugar until they turn light yellow.

In a pot over medium heat, warm the milk with the chile and arrowroot, stirring constantly for about 10 minutes, until it thickens. Remove the chile and very slowly pour the milk over the egg and sugar mixture, whisking slowly. Be careful not to let the eggs get too hot or they will scramble.

Return the mixture to the pot and, stirring constantly, bring to a boil over low heat. Cook for 1 to 2 minutes, until the cream thickens. Pass through a fine strainer into a bowl, add the mastic, and let cool to just warm. Add the yogurt and stir vigorously for a few seconds.

Let cool completely, placing the bowl in a larger container filled with ice cubes. Stir from time to time until completely cold. Place in an ice cream machine and freeze according to the manufacturer's instructions.

Note
Keep mastic in the freezer. It can be powdered easily in a mortar when frozen. Use a stone or porcelain mortar, because mastic sticks to wood.

✦ Oriental Orange "Cream" ✦

With no eggs or cream, this light fruity dessert is based on *portocal peltesi*, a Turkish recipe I tasted in Istanbul. You can make it with any fruit juice—lemon, tangerine, grape, pomegranate, or others. You can also use the fruit "cream" as filling for a prebaked tart shell. I like to serve it with cakes, as well as with Sweet Couscous with Orange Preserves, Sultanas, and Pistachios (page 200). Makes 6 servings

2 tablespoons grated orange zest

1 1/4 cups sugar, or more to taste

1/4 cup plus 2 tablespoons cornstarch

1 1/2 cups fresh orange juice

1/3 cup sweet white wine, preferably Samos

6 Dried Orange Slices (recipe follows) for garnish

Mix the zest and sugar together in a bowl and let stand for 1 to 2 hours at room temperature, stirring every now and then.

Pour 1 cup water over the sugar, add the cornstarch, and stir to dissolve. Transfer to a saucepan over medium heat and cook, stirring, until the sugar is completely dissolved, about 4 minutes. Add the orange juice and wine and continue stirring until the mixture thickens, about 6 minutes.

Pour into 6 individual glasses, let cool, and refrigerate for 4 hours or overnight. Top with the dried orange slices and serve.

Dried Orange Slices

With a special citrus knife or a sharp serrated knife, cut one or more oranges in half and cut each half into very thin slices. Spread the slices on a baking dish lined with parchment paper and place in a very low oven (about 180°F). Let the slices dry for 3 to 5 hours, depending on their thickness. Let cool and store in a bag in the freezer.

⋅ Fig and Yogurt Semifreddo ⋅

This is not a traditional recipe, but it came to me one August afternoon as Costas, my husband, brought me yet another basketful of figs from our trees. I had already made jams, both sweet and spicy, we had eaten more fresh ones than we could digest, and the refrigerator was filled with yet more figs from the previous days. I decided to freeze some, thinking that maybe I could make tarts in the winter. I sliced them and packed them in bags in the freezer. A few days later, as we were experimenting with our not-so-great ice cream maker, I remembered the frozen figs and thought that a fig and yogurt ice cream would be interesting. So I mashed them in the blender with some yogurt. The result was a wonderful thick semifrozen cream that didn't really need to go into the ice cream maker at all. A few adjustments—some ginger and brandy, to give it zest, and honey if your figs are not very sweet—and this extra-fast dessert was born.

Makes 4 or 5 servings

1^1/$_2$ pounds fresh black figs, not too ripe

^{1}/$_3$ cup Greek yogurt (whole-milk, low-fat, or nonfat), preferably sheep's milk (see page 213)

3 tablespoons honey, preferably thyme or lavender, or more to taste

1 to 1^1/$_2$ teaspoons grated fresh ginger, to taste

3 tablespoons brandy or dark rum (optional)

Thinly sliced fig preserves for serving (optional; see Note)

Wash, dry, and quarter the figs. Place in resealable plastic freezer bags and freeze for 3 hours or more.

Place the frozen figs, yogurt, honey, 1 teaspoon of the ginger, and the brandy if you're using it in a blender or food processor. Pulse to puree. Don't overwork the mixture. Taste and add more honey and/or ginger. Serve immediately in glasses, topped with sliced fig preserves if desired.

Note
Simmered in heavy syrup, whole green unripe figs become one of the popular Greek "spoon sweets." They can be purchased at fantisfoods.com or titanfood.com.

Ouzo-Scented Almond, Yogurt, and Olive Oil Cake

This recipe was inspired by a cake from the southern Peloponnese, an area that produces wonderful olive oil. Traditional Greek cakes—like the *karydopita* (walnut cake) served in most Greek restaurants all over the United States—are called *glyka tapsiou* ("pan sweets"). They are baked in large round or rectangular pans and doused in heavy syrup when cool. I make the cake in regular cake pans, adding crunchy almonds on the top and bottom. Makes two $8^1/2$-inch loaves

2 cups almonds

1 cup light olive oil, or $^1/2$ cup olive plus $^1/2$ cup sunflower oil, plus more for the pans

4 large eggs, separated

$1^1/2$ cups sugar, plus 2 or 3 tablespoons for sprinkling

$^3/4$ cup ouzo or Pernod

1 cup plus 2 tablespoons Greek yogurt, preferably sheep's milk (see page 213)

$3^1/2$ cups unbleached all-purpose flour

3 teaspoons baking powder

3 star anise, freshly ground in a spice or coffee grinder

$^1/2$ teaspoon sea salt

Preheat the oven to 375°F.

Arrange $1^1/2$ cups of the almonds on a baking sheet and lightly toast under the broiler, about 6 minutes. Grind, not too fine, and set aside. Coarsely grind the rest of the almonds and set aside separately.

Brush two $8^1/2$ X $4^1/2$ X $2^1/2$-inch loaf pans with oil and line the bottoms with parchment paper. Brush the paper with oil and sprinkle each with $1^1/2$ tablespoons of the untoasted almonds.

In a large bowl, beat the egg yolks and sugar with a handheld mixer until creamy and light colored. Add the oil and beat for 30 seconds. Add the ouzo and yogurt and mix for another 30 seconds.

In another bowl, stir together the flour, baking powder, star anise, salt, and toasted almonds.

Slowly add the liquids to the flour mixture, whisking with the handheld mixer at medium speed to incorporate.

Clean and dry the beaters. Beat the egg whites until stiff. With a spatula, carefully fold one-third of the egg whites into the cake mixture, then add another third, and when fully incorporated, fold in the rest.

Divide the batter between the pans and sprinkle with the remaining untoasted almonds. Sprinkle each pan with about 1 tablespoon sugar and place in the lower third of the oven. Bake for 1 hour or more, until golden brown and a tester inserted in the center comes out clean. Let cool on a rack for 15 minutes, then unmold and let cool completely before cutting. You can prepare the cake 1 day ahead, wrap in foil, and store at room temperature for up to 5 days.

✦ Sweet Couscous with Orange Preserves, ✦ Sultanas, and Pistachios

A kind of sweet grain pilaf, this dessert was inspired by a buttery sweet couscous that I tasted in Tunisia. I like to mix in some bulgur to give the soft store-bought couscous a more interesting flavor and texture. Serve with a dollop of thick creamy yogurt and extra orange preserves or with Oriental Orange "Cream" (page 196). If you refrigerate the couscous, it will become almost solid, so I suggest you prepare it only a few hours ahead and keep it at room temperature. Makes 6 servings

2^1/2 cups fresh orange juice, or more as needed

2 tablespoons honey

^{1}/4 cup sultanas (golden raisins)

1 cup couscous

^{1}/2 cup coarse bulgur, soaked in water for 30 minutes, drained, and spread on a clean tea towel

3 tablespoons orange or bitter orange preserves, or more to taste

^{2}/3 cup coarsely chopped shelled pistachios

^{1}/2 teaspoon ground cinnamon, or to taste

^{1}/2 teaspoon freshly ground white pepper, or to taste (optional)

2 to 3 tablespoons Grand Marnier or other orange-flavored liqueur (optional)

Strips of orange zest or Dried Orange Slices (page 196) for garnish

Combine 2 cups of the orange juice, the honey, and the sultanas in a saucepan and bring to a boil. Remove from the heat and stir in the couscous. Cover and set aside for 5 minutes. Add the bulgur, the rest of the orange juice, the orange preserves, half the pistachios, the cinnamon, pepper if you like, and liqueur if you're using it. Stir to mix well, cover, and let stand for another 5 to 10 minutes. Taste and add more preserves if you like. The mixture should be somewhat moist.

Spoon into individual bowls. Sprinkle with the remaining pistachios and decorate with orange zest or Dried Orange Slices. Serve at room temperature.

Dried Fig, Apricot, and Almond Balls

I'm sure you will love these little fruity balls, which were inspired by the first sweets cooks ever created. Mashed dried figs, mixed with honey and nuts, were one of the desserts ancient Greeks and Romans liked to eat while sipping their strong, sweet wines. In a similar vein, the Arabs have always loved their *hais,* a simple sweet made by kneading together chopped pitted dates and walnuts, pistachios, bread crumbs, and a little sesame oil. *Haroset* (or charoset), the traditional fruit and nut mixture served at the Jewish Passover, is a similar concoction. My variation on this theme is a combination of dried fruits, nuts, honey, and a little sweet wine. Serve after lunch or dinner, with coffee or tea.

Makes about 50

1 cup blanched and peeled almonds

1 cup walnuts

12 dried figs

24 good-quality dried apricots

$^1/_2$ teaspoon freshly grated nutmeg

$^2/_3$ teaspoon ground cinnamon

3 tablespoons honey, preferably thyme scented

2 to 4 tablespoons sweet white wine, preferably Samos, as needed

$^1/_2$ cup sesame seeds

15 to 20 Turkish bay leaves, fresh or dried (optional)

Place the almonds, walnuts, figs, and apricots in a food processor. Add the nutmeg, cinnamon, honey, and 2 tablespoons of the wine. Process, pulsing a couple of times and then letting the motor run continuously, until you have a homogenous sticky dough. If it is too hard, add a little more wine to facilitate the process.

One tablespoon at a time, shape the dough into balls by rolling it between your palms. Scrape your hands with a spatula when they become too sticky to continue or wet with some sweet wine if you like. Place the sesame seeds on a plate and briefly roll the finished fruit balls on the sesame seeds, pressing lightly so that a few seeds stick to the balls. Do not cover them completely with sesame seeds.

Place the balls on parchment paper and let sit, uncovered, for 4 to 5 hours or overnight. When serving, place each ball on a bay leaf. To store, pack in tins and keep in a dry, cool place. The confections will keep for about 2 months, although after 4 weeks they tend to become dry. If you plan to keep them longer, wrap each one individually in cellophane.

Sweet Couscous with Orange Preserves,
Sultanas, and Pistachios, page 200,
and Oriental Orange Cream, page 196

Dried Fig, Apricot, and
Almond Balls, page 201

Roasted Almond Cookies

Greeks call these delicate melt-in-your-mouth cookies *kourambiedes*. They are coated with confectioners' sugar and traditionally were prepared for Christmas. You can find similar cookies in various Middle Eastern countries, often sprinkled with rose water or citrus flower water before being rolled in confectioners' sugar. The old island recipes called for lard since butter was not a common ingredient of the Mediterranean countries. I have also found kourambiedes made entirely with olive oil. Today the cookies are prepared exclusively with butter, but I love this old lighter version. Makes 3 dozen

8 tablespoons lard or unsalted butter, softened

$1/2$ cup sunflower oil

$1/3$ cup confectioners' sugar, plus about 2 cups for sprinkling the cookies

1 egg yolk

Grated zest of 1 lemon

3 tablespoons ouzo, Pernod, or any other anise-flavored liqueur

3 cups unbleached all-purpose flour

$1^1/2$ teaspoons baking powder

$1/2$ to $2/3$ teaspoon freshly ground white pepper (optional)

1 cup coarsely ground toasted almonds (see page 213)

Beat the lard and sunflower oil in a food processor or electric mixer with $1/3$ cup confectioners' sugar for about 6 minutes. Add the egg yolk, lemon zest, and ouzo and process for 2 to 3 minutes more. Sift the flour with the baking powder and pepper if you're using it. Fit the processor with a dough hook and gradually add the flour mixture. Process the mixture for 2 to 3 minutes, until a soft dough forms. Add the almonds and process until the dough is smooth again, 1 to 2 minutes more.

Preheat the oven to 350°F.

Shape tablespoons of dough into round, oval, or crescent-shaped cookies and place on a cookie sheet, leaving about 1 inch between the cookies so they won't stick together as they expand. Bake for 20 to 25 minutes, until very pale golden. Cool for 10 minutes. Spread 1 cup confectioners' sugar on a large serving plate. Very carefully, because they break easily, roll a cookie in the sugar and place on a rack to cool. Proceed with all the cookies, adding more sugar to the plate as necessary. Finally, sift additional sugar on top of the cookies and let rest for 3 to 4 hours or overnight. Carefully pack the cookies in boxes, spreading sheets of wax paper between layers. The cookies will keep for 2 months or longer.

✦ Honey-Infused Spice Cookies ✦

These traditional Greek cookies, flavored with thyme-scented honey, orange juice and zest, brandy, cinnamon, and cloves, are traditionally prepared for Christmas. The recipe is my mother's, passed to her from her mother. The deep flavor of these cookies, called *melomakarona* in Greek, actually improves with time. Serve after dinner with coffee and sweet wine. Makes 60 to 70 cookies

1$^1/4$ cups light olive oil or half olive oil and half canola or safflower oil

$^1/3$ cup sugar

1 cup fresh orange juice

3 to 4 cups unbleached all-purpose flour

2$^1/2$ teaspoons baking powder

$^1/2$ cup brandy

1$^1/2$ cups fine semolina

Grated zest of 1 orange

Grated zest of 1 lemon

$^1/2$ teaspoon ground cloves

1 teaspoon ground cinnamon

$^1/2$ teaspoon freshly ground black pepper

FOR THE HONEY SYRUP

1 cup sugar

1 cup honey

A large piece of orange peel

A large piece of lemon peel

1 cup coarsely ground walnuts

1 teaspoon ground cloves

1 teaspoon ground cinnamon

Using an electric mixer, beat the olive oil with the sugar in a large bowl. Add the orange juice. In a separate bowl, mix 2 cups of the flour with the baking powder. Gradually beat the flour mixture into the oil mixture. Add the brandy, semolina, orange and lemon zests, cloves, cinnamon, and pepper, beating at low speed.

Turn the mixture out onto a floured surface and start kneading, adding more flour as necessary, until you have a soft, elastic dough. Cover the dough with plastic wrap and let it rest for about 30 minutes.

Preheat the oven to 350°F.

Break off tablespoons of dough, roll them in your hands, then shape them into oval cookies about 2 inches long. Press the top of each cookie with the tines of a fork to make a decorative pattern. Place the cookies on baking sheets and bake for 20 to 25 minutes, until light brown. Let them cool completely overnight on a rack, which allows them to harden enough so they don't got too crumbly in the syrup.

The next day, make the honey syrup. In a saucepan, combine the sugar, honey, and

2 cups water. Bring to a boil. Add the orange and lemon peels and simmer for 5 to 10 minutes to let the flavors blend. Turn the heat to very low to keep the syrup liquid. Place 2 or 3 cookies on a large slotted spoon and dip them into the syrup. Don't let them soak in it—they should absorb some syrup and remain crunchy.

Place a layer of honey-dipped cookies on a dish. Combine the walnuts with the ground cloves and cinnamon, then sprinkle the mixture over the cookies. Repeat with the rest of the cookies. Let them cool completely before serving. The cookies keep well for 3 weeks, stored in an airtight container.

✦ Greek Easter Bread Biscotti ✦

Greek Easter bread *(tsoureki)* is very similar to the Jewish challah and to Italian panettone, but it contains less fat and more spices. In many Athenian bakeries tsoureki is sliced and baked again to make these wonderful, very light biscotti. Serve with coffee or tea or use as a base for English trifle or bread pudding.

Makes about 8 dozen biscotti

$^1/4$ cup warm milk

2 tablespoons honey

$1^1/2$ tablespoons active dry yeast

4 tablespoons unsalted butter, softened

$^1/4$ cup sugar

2 tablespoons olive oil

$^1/4$ cup fresh orange juice

1 teaspoon ground mastic

1 teaspoon ground mahlep

$^1/4$ cup grated orange zest

3 eggs, separated

4 to 5 cups unbleached all-purpose flour, as needed

$^1/2$ teaspoon salt

2 tablespoons cold milk for brushing the loaves

Combine the warm milk and 1 tablespoon of the honey in a small bowl. Add the yeast and allow to dissolve.

In another bowl, beat the butter with the sugar and remaining honey. Add the olive oil, orange juice, mastic, mahlep, and orange zest. Continue beating while adding the eggs, one by one, reserving $^1/2$ egg yolk.

Sift 4 cups of the flour with the salt and make a well in the center. Pour in the yeast and butter mixtures and stir to form a dough. Knead with your hands for about 10 minutes, adding a little more flour if the dough is too sticky or warm milk if it is too hard. (Alternatively, work the dough for 3 to 4 minutes in a food processor or an electric mixer fitted with the dough hook.)

When the dough becomes soft and shiny, form it into a ball and place it in an oiled bowl. Turn the dough so that is is covered with oil, cover with plastic wrap, and let rise for about 2 hours, until doubled in size.

When doubled in size, punch the dough down and divide into 3 equal pieces. Roll each piece into a loaf about 15 inches long.

(continued)

Place the loaves on a baking sheet lined with parchment paper and cover with oiled plastic wrap. Let rise for another 2 hours, until almost doubled in size.

Preheat the oven to 375°F.

Beat the remaining $1/2$ egg yolk with the cold milk and brush the mixture on the loaves. Bake for 30 to 40 minutes, until nicely browned. Let cool on a rack.

Turn the oven down to 175° to 200°F. Using a very good bread knife, cut the loaves into $1/2$-inch slices and place them on a cookie and return to the oven for 2 to 3 hours, until dry. Let cool completely on a rack and store in airtight tins. The biscotti will keep for up to 6 months.

✦ Strawberry Ratafia ✦

Argyro Barbarigou Papadakis, the owner and cook of the eponymous very successful fish restaurant in Athens, offers this wonderfully aromatic drink to her patrons at the end of the meal. It is an ideal way to conclude a highly flavored lunch or dinner, and since I got the basic recipe I've made it in bulk whenever I get the best fragrant strawberries or peaches (see the variation). Argyro calls it "liqueur," but it is what the French call *ratafia* (pronounced rha-tah-fee-AH): the fresh juice of grapes or other fruit, mixed with alcohol that prevents fermentation and preserves the fruit flavor and aroma.

Makes about $1^1/2$ quarts

1 pound ripe but not mushy strawberries, preferably organic, hulled

1 cup sugar, or more to taste

$3^1/4$ cups vodka

Halve the largest strawberries and put all the berries in a blender with the sugar. Blend for 30 seconds or more, until you get a smooth puree. Stir in the vodka and pour into bottles. Cover and chill in the refrigerator for 8 hours or overnight. Shake and serve in shot glasses. Strawberry ratafia keeps in the refrigerator for 3 months or longer. Its stunning color gets darker, but it remains fruity even after a year.

PEACH RATAFIA
Substitute $1^1/2$ pounds ripe and fragrant peaches, peeled and pitted, for the strawberries, adding about $1/2$ cup sugar or to taste. If you want, pass the peach pulp through a fine strainer, pouring the vodka over the solids as you press them through the strainer.

APPENDIX

Precooking Beans, Chickpeas, and Wheat Berries

If you love pulses, as do all the inhabitants of the Mediterranean Basin, you may feel frustrated every time you feel like making a dish with beans or chickpeas and discover that you need to start a day in advance, soaking them before you proceed to cook them for about an hour, to make your favorite dish. Although you can get canned chickpeas and beans, for me there is no comparison to the taste of the pulses you cook from scratch. That's why I propose that you precook and freeze some beans and chickpeas to have on hand every time you feel like whipping up a tasty hummus (page 65), Fettuccine with Chickpeas and Peperoncini (page 163), or Bigilla, the Maltese spicy mashed bean spread (page 63). The instructions are based on what my mother has taught me and on Aliza Green's wonderful book *Beans*.

Makes about 6 cups cooked beans or chickpeas, enough for 6 to 8 people

2 cups dried beans, such as giant or large lima beans, coco blanc, cannellini, pinto, navy, or a combination, and/or chickpeas (1 pound)

Soak the beans and/or chickpeas in separate large bowls in enough cold water to come at least 3 inches above the beans. Let stand for 10 to 12 hours. Cannellini, pinto, and navy beans need less soaking (6 to 8 hours), but you can leave them all to soak overnight.

FOR BEANS

The next morning, rinse the beans under cold water, place in a large pot, and cover with water ($4^1/2$ to 5 quarts). Bring to a boil over medium heat, cook for 5 minutes, drain in a colander, and rinse well with warm running water. Rinse the pot, put back the beans, and cover with cold or just warm water, adding fresh sprigs of thyme, oregano, or savory or 3 or 4 dried bay leaves if you like. Bring to a boil, lower the heat, and simmer the beans for 1 hour or more, until soft. Taste after 1 hour and then after 20 minutes, making sure the beans are almost cooked and soft but not mushy.

Drain, discard the herbs, let cool completely, and store in sealed bags in the freezer.

FOR CHICKPEAS

The next morning, rinse the chickpeas under cold water, place in a large pot, and cover with water ($4^1/2$ to 5 quarts). Bring to a boil over medium heat, cook for 5 minutes, drain in a colander, and rinse well with warm running water. Rinse the pot, put back the chickpeas, and cover with cold or just warm water, adding $1/2$ teaspoon baking soda and fresh sprigs of thyme, oregano, or savory or 3 or 4 dried bay leaves if you like. Bring to a boil, lower the heat, and simmer the chickpeas for $1^1/2$ hours or more, until soft. Taste after $1^1/2$ hours and then after 20 minutes, making sure the chickpeas are almost cooked and soft but not mushy.

Drain, discard the herbs, let cool completely, and store in sealed bags in the freezer.

FOR WHEAT BERRIES (GRANO)

Choose the reddish, hard (high-protein) wheat berries, also called *grano*. These are the ones used in southern Italy, Greece, and the Middle East. Unlike pearl barley these are not "polished" but whole, unprocessed kernels that need soaking and long cooking, much like beans. Their incomparable earthy and nutty flavor is ample compensation for the extra work. Soak, cook, and store in the freezer a pound of wheat berries to have on hand and add to rice pilafs, salads, stuffings, meat, or vegetable stews or to eat for breakfast or as a snack, mixed with yogurt and fruit or honey.

Soak $2^2/3$ cups (1 pound) hard reddish wheat berries for 2 to 3 hours or rinse under warm water for 3 minutes. Place in a large pot and cover with water ($4^1/2$ to 5 quarts). Bring to a boil, lower the heat, and simmer for about 35 minutes. Taste, and if still hard, continue cooking and taste again after 5 to 10 minutes, making sure the wheat berries are almost cooked but al dente, not mushy. Drain and cool completely. Store in sealed bags in the freezer. One pound of uncooked wheat berries yields 7 to 8 cups cooked, enough for 6 to 8 people.

Raw, Half-Cooked, and Baked Tomatoes

In late summer or early fall, when irresistible, fragrant vine-ripened heirloom tomatoes fill the stands of your farmers' market, preserve their tasty flesh to use in special sauces, stews, and soups all year. You won't believe how invigorating and complex their flavor is, even compared with the most expensive imported canned tomatoes. Tomatoes baked in olive oil, often called *confit,* are very attractive and pack a deeply concentrated tomato flavor. They are infinitely better than the salty and leathery sun-dried tomatoes and make an ideal topping for flat breads and tarts and a wonderful addition to pasta, bulgur, soups, and winter salads.

GRATING TOMATOES

Instead of blanching, peeling, and chopping tomatoes, as classic French cooking suggests, Mediterranean cooks grate the tomatoes with a box grater to get the tomato pulp. The seeds are not discarded, because they are particularly flavorful.

Halve each tomato vertically, cut off and discard the stem, and carefully grate on a large-holed grater, cut side facing the holes. Discard the skin, which will remain in your hand.

FRESH TOMATO PULP

Measure 1 or 2 cups of the grated tomato flesh and freeze in shallow trays lined with plastic wrap for about 3 hours. Make sure the frozen tomatoes are about $^1/2$ inch thick or less. This way they will melt and cook faster and you can even cut the pieces in half if you want to use less. Take the frozen pulp out of the trays, break it into chunks, and store in resealable plastic bags in the freezer.

HALF-COOKED TOMATO PULP

You will need less of this more-concentrated tomato pulp to flavor foods. In a nonreactive saucepan, bring the grated tomatoes to a boil and cook over medium heat for 15 to 20 minutes. Let cool and freeze as above.

BAKED TOMATOES (ALSO CALLED TOMATO CONFIT)

Halve the tomatoes and arrange cut side up in one layer on a shallow baking sheet lined with parchment paper. Drizzle with olive oil and sprinkle with some sea salt. Bake at 275°F for 2 to 3 hours, depending on the size of the tomatoes, until very soft and about a third of their original size. You can bake 2 or 3 sheets at a time, changing their position every 30 to 40 minutes, or cook on convection setting (no need to move the sheets). Let the tomatoes cool completely and freeze in sealed bags.

Toasting Seeds and Nuts

FOR SEEDS AND PINE NUTS

Warm a skillet over medium-high heat and toast the seeds or pine nuts, turning with a spatula until just golden, about 3 minutes. Be careful, because the pine nuts especially burn easily.

ALMONDS, HAZELNUTS, OR WALNUTS

Preheat the oven to 375°F. Put the nuts on a baking sheet and toast, tossing once with a spatula until just colored and fragrant, 3 to 5 minutes, being careful not to burn them.

Draining Yogurt

If you can't get the thick Greek yogurt a recipe may ask for, drain regular yogurt.

Makes 1 cup
1²/3 cups whole-milk yogurt

Line a strainer with double cheesecloth and set it over a large bowl. Add the yogurt, cover with plastic wrap, and let drain overnight in the refrigerator.

The slightly sour but very tasty and nourishing liquid left in the bowl after draining the yogurt adds flavor to vegetable stews and stocks. Keep it in a jar in the refrigerator or, better yet, freeze it to use when you need it.

Pitting Olives

To remove the pits from olives you want to chop, place a handful at a time in a resealable plastic bag, seal the bag, and lay it on the work surface. Beat the olives with a meat mallet or a rolling pin to crack them. Remove the olives from the bag, discard the pits, and chop them or mash them in the blender.

SOURCES

The majority of the ingredients for the recipes are available at your local farmers' market, in supermarkets, and in various ethnic and Middle Eastern grocery stores across the United States. Here are some sources for best-quality spices and other foods that may be difficult to find in your neighborhood.

Adriana's Bazaar
321 Grand Central Terminal
New York, NY 10017
(800) 316-0820
Aleppo pepper, salt-packed capers from Spain, a large variety of spices, mastic, and bulgur; catalog available

Balducci's
(800) 225-3822
www.balduccis.com
Greek, Italian, and French olives, salt-packed capers (in store only); catalog available

Bob's Red Mill Natural Foods
5209 SE International Way
Milwaukie, OR 97222
www.bobsredmill.com
Wheat berries, barley grits, organic flours, and legumes

Buon Italia
75 Ninth Avenue
New York, NY 10011
(212) 633-9090
Fax: (212) 633-9717
www.buonitalia.com,
e-mail: info@buonitalia.com
Imports the much-praised salted menaica anchovies

The Cook's Garden
P.O. Box 535
Londonderry, VT 05148
(802) 824-5526
Fax: (802) 824-9556
Seeds for vegetables and exotic greens; catalog available

Dean & DeLuca
560 Broadway
New York, NY 10012
(800) 999-0306
www.deananddeluca.com
Greek oregano and other herbs from Crete, coarse (# 3) bulgur, cheeses from all over the Mediterranean; catalog available

Ethnic Grocer
www.ethnicgrocer.com
Coarse bulgur, spices, olive oils, olives, and other Greek products

Formaggio Kitchen
244 Huron Avenue
Cambridge, MA 02138
(888) 212-3224; (617) 354-4750
Fax: (617) 547-5680
120 Essex Street
Essex Street Market
New York, NY 10002
(212) 982-8200
www.formaggiokitchen.com
Aleppo, Maraş, and Urfa peppers, Italian and Greek cheeses, olive oils, etc.

Fresca Italia Inc.
200 Valley Dr. #14
Brisbane, CA 94005
(415) 468-9800
Fax: (415) 468-9900
www.frescaitalia.com,
e-mail: info@frescaitalia.com
Unusual Italian cheeses and delicacies from various regions

Greek Olive Warehouse Imports, Inc.
5340 W. Montrose Avenue
Chicago, IL 60641
Fax: 1-773-792-6388
www.greekolivewarehouse.com/mich10shmi14.html
Olives and olive oils, as well as oregano sprigs, mountain tea, Kalamata figs

Greenleaf
1955 Jerrold Avenue
San Francisco, CA 94124
(415) 647-2991
Fax: (415) 647-2996
Wild greens

Gustiamo
www.gustiamo.com
Italian sardines, tuna, colatura de alici, sausages, and dried fruits

Haig's Delicacies
642 Clement Street
San Francisco, CA 94118
(415) 752-6283
Fax: (415) 752-6177
www.haigsdelicacies.com,
e-mail: haigs@aol.com
Fresh phyllo pastry, bulgur, spices, and basturma

Indian Rock Produce
530 California Road
Quakertown, PA 18951
(800) 882-0512; (215) 536-9600
Fax: (215) 529-9447
Fresh produce; newsletter available

Italfoods
P.O. Box 2563
205 Shaw Road
South San Francisco, CA 94080-6605
(650) 877-0724
Fax: (650) 871-9437
www.italfoodsinc.com/regionDetails.asp?region=calabria
Imports the Tutto Calabria brand; pickled peperoncini, hot sauces, and spreads from Calabria; available in many food shops and at Amazon.com

Kalustyan's
123 Lexington Avenue
New York, NY 10016
(212) 685-3451
Fax: (212) 683-8458
www.kalustyans.com
Aleppo pepper, spices, coarse bulgur, barley, couscous, falafel shaper; catalog available

King Arthur Flour
P.O. Box 876
Norwich, VT 05055
(800) 827-6836
www.kingarthurflour.com
Barley flour; catalog available

La Tienda
www.tienda.com/food/products/se-28.html
Spanish products: marinated anchovies (boquerones), salted cod, chorizo, ñoras (the densely flavored dried peppers), roasted piquillo peppers (for salads)

The Mastiha Shop
145 Orchard Street
New York, NY
(212) 253-0895
e-mail: info@mastihashopny.com
Mastic crystals, spoon sweet (fruit preserves), and other products from the east Mediterranean

Old Chatham Sheep Dairy
155 Shaker Road
Old Chatham, NY 12136
(518) 794-7726, ext. 9
Sheep's milk yogurt

Penzeys
(800) 741-7787
Fax: (410) 760-7317
www.penzeys.com
Spices, paprika

Seeds of Change
www.seedsofchange.com
Organic and heirloom seeds for chiles, herbs, and vegetables

Spanish Table
www.spanishtable.com
Ñoras and other spices, like piment d'espelette, pimentón (smoked paprika), etc.

The Spice Hunter
P.O. Box 8110
San Luis Obispo, CA 93403-8110
(800) 444-3061
Fax: (800) 444-3096
www.spicehunter.com,
e-mail: consumerline@spicehunter.com
Greek oregano

Sultan's Delight
P.O. Box 090302
Brooklyn, NY 11209
(800) 852-5046
Mahlep, mastic, and other Middle Eastern ingredients; catalog available

Sunnyland Mills
4469 E. Annadale Avenue
Fresno, CA 93725-2221
(800) 501-8017
Fax: (559) 233-6431
wwwlsunnylandmills.com
For coarse bulgur and wheat berries (grano)

Theodorou Salt Industry
www.sailorsalt.com/site/content/view/23/46/
Plain and flavored sea salt flakes from Cyprus

Titan Foods
www.titanfood.com
Great selection of Greek and imported foods, including paximadia (savory barley biscuits) from Crete, spices, mastic, excellent olives, and imported frozen prepared foods

World Spice Merchants
www.worldspice.com
Aleppo pepper and all kinds of other spices

Zingerman's
1220 Jewett
Ann Arbor, MI 48104
(888) 636-8162
Salt-packed capers, olive oils, olives from all over the Mediterranean, artisanal Mediterranean and Greek cheeses; catalog available

INDEX

ABOUT THE AUTHOR

Aglaia Kremezi was born in Athens and has lived on Kea, an island in the Cyclades, since 1999. She is the author of more than half a dozen books in English and Greek, including *The Foods of Greece,* which won the IACP Julia Child Award. She is a journalist, writer, photographer, and food columnist for the Sunday Athens paper *Kyriakatiki Eleftherotypia* and has been published in the *Los Angeles Times, Gourmet, Bon Appétit, Food and Wine, Food Arts, BBC Good Food,* and other publications. She has appeared on *Good Morning America, CBS This Morning,* and other television shows in the United States. She often lectures at the Culinary Institute at Greystone in Napa, California, and has taught at Macy's Degustibus, at the French Culinary Institute in New York, and at many other cooking schools around the country.

With a group of friends, she created Kea Artisanal, www.keartisanal.com, a cooking school and cultural program on Kea. She is an authority on the history of ancient Greek and Mediterranean cuisines and has made presentations at many international conferences on food. She is a consultant for Molyvos, one of the first upscale Greek restaurants in New York City, which was awarded three stars by Ruth Reichl of the *New York Times.* Her Web site is www.aglaiakremezi.com.